A HANDBOOK OF
SMALL BOAT CRUISING

A HANDBOOK
OF
SMALL
BOAT CRUISING

Fox Geen

DAVID & CHARLES : NEWTON ABBOT

TO SLIM

0 7153 6096 5

© Fox Green 1973

First published 1973
Second impression 1975
Third impression 1977

Printed in Great Britain by
Redwood Burn Limited, Trowbridge & Esher

Contents

Contents

List of Illustrations

7

List of Illustrations

Foreword

There is little new to be said about getting around in small boats. I have just tried to set out simply the elements of what mediocre competence has kept me out of the more serious kinds of trouble for longer than I care to think about. Hopefully concise and comprehensive, this book is offered with diffidence, for in the writing I found out how little I really do know of a vast subject. Other and better books abound but there may come moments, notably in times of stress, when you may find theory and practice hard to correlate. Perhaps a reference volume like this one may be useful at such times.

Much of what appears in Chapters One and Three appeared at some time in the pages of *Practical Boat Owner*. In acknowledging this I owe a debt of gratitude to the editor of that journal, and my friend, Denny Desoutter. Without his kindness and practical encouragement this book would probably have remained unwritten.

CHAPTER ONE

Boat Handling

WIND AND WATER

Aside from the simple mechanics of being able to take a boat out and bring her back in one piece there are many things to be mastered if you aspire to be a reasonably competent sailor. One of these is boat handling—the multitude of actions to be taken before setting and after lowering sail, or operating the throttle of a powercraft, and often in between. It is part and parcel of the business of getting about and should be carried out with assurance, in safety and with a minimum of inconvenience to other folk and their property.

Vessels afloat are subjected to the pressures of moving air on their topsides, rigging and sails, and the water upon immersed parts of the hull. Helpful or obstructive, the *effect* of these forces must be understood if we are to take advantage of them in controlling our boats. They need careful consideration at times of transition from a state of immobility to one of motion and vice versa.

What is likely to happen during those critical moments after casting off before the boat is fully in command and properly under way? How slowly, and at what angle, should I close that jetty, and what will happen when the headline is made fast and the jib let fly, or throttle cut?

Driving a car is simple in comparison, for once it is stopped and braked it remains motionless in relation to its terrain. A driver making a U-turn can predict where he will end up. A helmsman ought to be able to do so, but he must allow for the effects of wind and stream, over which he has no control, as well as the correct handling of tiller and sheets, or throttle and wheel.

Practical experience is essential, but it helps to have knowledge of the basic principles involved in boat handling. Also to get into the habit of working things out from these first principles, as this makes mistakes less likely than if sophisticated methods are employed. These may be quicker and neater for the adept, but when you are tired and harassed, it is best to use methods which make the least demands on the mind.

Take the case of a boat sailing at 2kn through the water directly into a 2kn stream (Fig 1). Ignore wind speed and direction for now, as we are only concerned with their *effect* upon the boat's behaviour, which is under helmsman's control. Rate and set of stream cannot be so ignored because their effect is to carry the vessel along bodily at the same speed and in the same direction.

I make a dot on the paper (1) to show my present position and argue thus. I am heading in *that* direction under wind effects in isolation. The dot (2) made at the end of a line 2in long will represent my position at the end of 1hr at 2kn. Now, assume that I had started out from point (2) and let the stream in isolation act on my boat for 1hr, where would I end up? I draw another line 2in long in the direction of the set of stream and end up at point (3), which can be seen to coincide exactly with point (1). I have, under the combined effects of wind and stream, not moved at all. This is perfectly obvious, but the important thing is that we have employed the basic principle of taking the wind and stream effects *separately* to ascertain their *combined* effect.

Fig 2 is similarly worked and shows a final position some way from the point of departure (1). Irrespective of the *heading* of the boat, she will have travelled over the seabed in the direction (1)–(3), known as her *track*. Chapter 2 explains how to calculate such things as the distance and direction of a track, but for now it is enough to understand that a combination of wind and stream effects can cause a boat to sail at an angle to her heading. A period

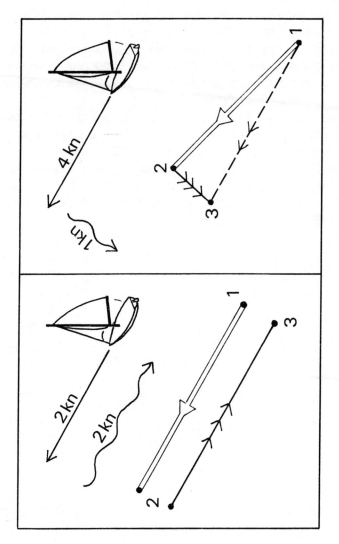

Fig 1 · Effect of wind and water—I   Fig 2 Effect of wind and water—II

of 1hr has been used as an example but it is essential to realise that wind and stream, whether singly or combined, have an instantaneous effect; at any given moment they will be influencing a vessel to move in a certain direction.

This fact has application to such matters as picking up a mooring, for which purpose you should ideally bring your boat close alongside and stationary *in relation to the buoy*. This calls for forethought—consider Fig 3.

Under main- and foresail you are running at 4kn directly into a stream of 1kn and want to pick up the buoy. It is easy to assume that speed can be reduced to 1kn under wind effect, which would be cancelled out by the 1kn stream, leaving the boat stationary at the buoy. A little thought will prove that this cannot be done with the mainsail up, so let us lower it. Now the jib can be eased

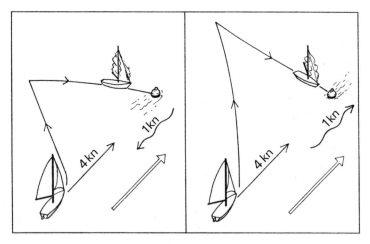

Fig 3 Approaching a buoy

to slow the boat and let fly to come to a halt. However, in any weight of wind it will flail about and, as soon as the wind effect is removed, the boat will start to gather sternway in the stream.

It is far better to approach the buoy at an angle, as illustrated.

Sheets and helm can be used to sail slowly and under full control along a track terminating at the buoy. The boat can then be held stationary for long enough to lift the mooring.

Carrying the argument a little further, imagine you are running at 4kn but this time the 1kn stream is flowing in the same direction. It will be impossible to halt at the buoy, even with all sail off, as you will be carried bodily past in the stream. So, sail on downwind of the buoy, change course and approach it into the stream at an angle, as in the previous case. Two important points are brought out:

1. To bring a boat stationary in relation to a fixed object it should be headed into the stream. Sails or motor must be used to keep the boat moving in the direction and speed which will oppose and finally cancel the stream effect;
2. Once the motive force of sails or motor is removed the boat will *immediately* start to gather way. This is one of the difficult times of transition previously mentioned.

Failure to grasp and act upon these two facts can cause frustration and damage. A boat must be kept under full control at all times.

Visual aids

If he wishes to use a stream to his advantage, a helmsman will find out all he can about its rate (speed) and set (direction). To the observant eye there are many indications about (Fig 4).

There is a good tip for taking advantage of the flow in a river or narrow channel. Here the water will be shallower nearer the banks than in midstream. Wind against tide exaggerates waves, and wind over tide smoothes them out. In a channel water flows faster where it is deep. So, if waves or ripples are more pronounced in midstream, the flow will be *against* the wind; if the middle of the channel is less bobbly than the borders, wind is over stream. This knowledge can be used when making way against the stream either up- or down-channel. As long as the water is deep enough, it will pay to stay in that part of the channel in which the stream flows more slowly. Thus, with the wind ahead, stay in the rougher water; with a following wind stay in the smooth.

Observation of indicators helps you to determine the set of a stream, but only experience can help in assessing its rate. No simple formula or guide exists and stream rates can be very deceptive. If danger exists, it will pay to anchor off temporarily

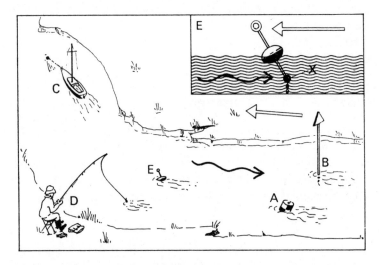

Fig 4 Indications of streams

A Waves ahead and eddies astern of channel buoy
B Wake astern of perch
C Anchored boat heading into stream
D Float downstream of fisherman, though his line is blowing out downwind
E Inclination of danbuoy. Watch this one—the inset shows why the buoy inclines into the stream

to measure the rate of flow. With the boat anchored, a speedometer will register the speed at which the water is flowing past. Other devices exist, such as the 'floating chip', which give tolerably accurate answers.

Simple measurement of speed

The 'floating chip' method described here can be used either to measure the rate of a stream or the speed of a boat through the water, for these are in fact the same thing. It is useful to know about if you do not have a speedometer.

It is necessary to measure a length, call it 20ft, along the deck of your boat and mark its ends; the distance can conveniently lie between two stanchions. Two men, a stopwatch and a small piece of wood complete the tally. One man stands near the forward mark and throws the chip ahead and clear of the bow wave. As it floats abeam of the mark, he starts the watch. When it gets abeam of the aft mark, the observer calls out or signals and the watch is stopped. A simple calculation gives the required speed, and it is an easy matter to construct a table to cover the boat's speed range if it is intended to use the method frequently.

If D is the measured length and T the elapsed time, in feet and seconds respectively, the speed in knots is given sufficiently accurately by the formula:

$$\frac{3D}{5T}$$

Thus a length of 20ft and a time of 3sec would give a speed of

$$\frac{3 \times 20}{5 \times 3} = 4\text{kn.}$$

Keeping on track

It is simple enough to draw a diagram of the effect of natural forces on the track of a boat, but in restricted waters practice is a matter of observation and experience. The main aids used are *transits*. Fig 5 illustrates their use.

As long as the tree on the riverbank stays in line with the spire, the boat is following a track which would, if extended, pass through both objects. If the view changes, as shown in inset A,

the vessel will be tracking downstream of the proper line, and, if
as in B, upstream. Correction will have to be made to the vessel's
heading to get back on to the right track and again to stay on it.
It is clear that any change of heading will vary the wind effect

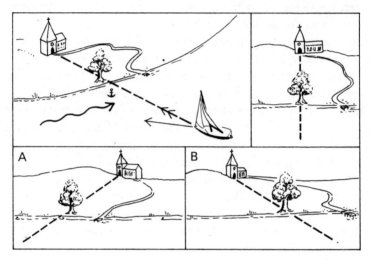

Fig 5 Following a transit line. Top right, correct transit. Too far
downstream (A) and too far upstream (B)

on the boat, thus affecting its speed. This can alter the combined
effect of wind and water being experienced previously and will
have to be taken into account when manoeuvring, especially at
close quarters. It all boils down to a question of experience based
on observation.

When you are approaching a buoy amid a horde of other moored
craft, their masts can usefully be made the basis of a succession
of transits. It is invaluable to be able to sail along a transit line
when nearing a quay or jetty ,where eddies can cause sudden and
significant changes to the waterflow.

Bearings
If transits cannot be found, a handbearing compass can be used

to stay on track by taking a succession of bearings of a single object such as a landfall buoy, anchored steamer or a mark ashore. Deviation from track will become quickly apparent, and the expedient is most useful at night, when objects ashore or close inshore may be invisible and a safe track can be followed using a single light. More details of the use of bearings follow in Chapter 2.

Practice
Surprisingly few yachtsmen regularly keep their hand in at such things as approaching and lifting a buoy, establishing and using transits, using the handbearing compass and generally teaching themselves how to take the best advantage of natural forces. This is remiss, for many a pleasant and interesting hour spent in this way might pay handsome dividends later. Should a contingency arise and you find yourself lacking in knowledge and skill, it may be too late. One only has to note the number of muffed or clumsy mooring pick-ups to realise that the owners of these boats would be in dire trouble if they had to deal with a man overboard. It is imperative to practise a routine for this emergency, dealt with in Chapter 5, and practice at picking up fenders, lifebuoys and the like will highlight the snags to be met with in even benevolent conditions and sheltered waters.

Powerboat owners have delicate control over their craft, and it should be a matter of pride for a sailing man to be able to handle his boat under sail alone with equal facility. It would be silly purism to contend that motors should not be used in some circumstances—crowded harbours, for example—but what happens if they fail, as is not unknown? There is also an uncommon satisfaction in bringing one's boat neatly, quietly and accurately to a standstill close aboard a chosen objective.

MOORINGS
The word 'way' is used in connection with the movement of a boat through the water, and should not be confused with 'weigh-

ing' an anchor, ie getting it out of the ground. A boat is said to make way, lose way, get under way, have no way on, have steerage way and so on. What is important from the point of boat handling is to know how much way your vessel carries. The ability to carry way is individual to any vessel, and means, simply, how far she will travel when propulsion ceases. It results from factors related to weight and resistance.

Weight, also called displacement, is the total weight of a boat and her cargo and equals the weight of water she displaces. Underwater resistance to motion is offered by the shape, area and smoothness of the immersed part of the hull. Windage is the resistance offered to the air mass by rigging, spars and other topside structures.

A dinghy will lose all way almost immediately she turns into wind, whereas a supertanker will carry her way for a distance measurable in miles. A mathematical comparison can be made between the ability of the two to carry their way, but the only practical resort of a helmsman is to find out the characteristics of his own boat by experimenting—preferably in open water where misjudgement will not matter.

Controllability
Ideal conditions seldom exist. Moorings come in clusters and are crowded, while buoys bob about and are difficult to secure even if you are stationary and within easy reach. To prevent over-shooting or falling short, and to allow for the intransigence of buoys, it is frequently necessary to increase or reduce speed rapidly. Powercraft are easily controlled, but easing sheets and spilling the wind of a sailing craft are unseamanlike expedients to use habitually. It will often be better to lower either main- or foresail beforehand, assuming that your boat is reasonably manoeuvrable under a single sail. Many are not, and better control can be achieved by backing a foresail to the required degree. A backed foresail can reduce speed or even induce sternway; the use of a fully backed foresail and carefully trim-

med main will enable a boat to be hove-to. This means that it is brought virtually to a standstill in the water. Most boats will heave-to successfully. Some lie quietly with tiller free; many with it lashed a'lee; and others with it lashed amidships or up to weather. A few will carry no headway, while others will forereach (sail ahead). If you are forced to heave-to in bad weather, it will be vital to know how fast and in what direction your boat will drift. It is better to find out in favourable circumstances than in an emergency.

Rapid reduction of headway
There are times when a rapid reduction of speed is urgent and impossible by sail handling alone. The effect of dragging a bucket over the stern is dramatic, but it must be stout and securely belayed to a strongpoint. Almost anything which will cause a drag in the water can be used in straits—oars, canvas covers, floorboards, etc—but they may be damaged and pull adrift, so think hard before using valuable items like sails.

Types of mooring
What lies below an innocent-looking mooring buoy is a matter for conjecture. Some of the arrangements met with, but by no means all, are depicted in Fig 6.

A rope pennant is simply there to bring up the chain and should not be used for making fast. Often these lines are in a poor state of health and will take little strain.

When a boat arrives at the buoy, that buoy has to be lifted to get at the pennant and then the chain. If it has a handle, the bowman may be able to grab it by reaching through pulpit or rails, but the most efficient way is to sweep below the buoy with a boathook and fetch out the pennant or riser. The chandler's boathook is not much good for the task; it is far better to use a large crook on the end of a shaft. One can be bent from mild steel, or better still a stainless rod, and securely seized in place. Varnished shafts are too slippery to be of use—it is best to use an

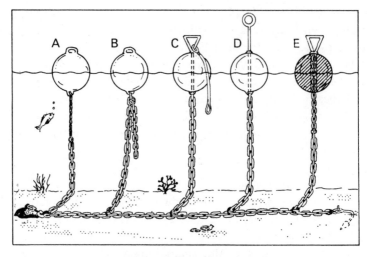

Fig 6 Types of mooring

A Mooring chain brought aboard using rope riser
B Mooring chain brought aboard with its buoy
C Buoy stays afloat, boat moored by strop
D Boat's own strop to buoy's ring
E Mooring chain brought aboard through buoy

ash pole and treat it with linseed oil. A mansize turk's head made on the end will prevent the pole slipping out of your hand.

Once hooked in, the important thing is to get the chain inboard and *belay* it smartly. Do not fuss about with getting the buoy aboard yet—they are tiresome to wheedle through pulpits—and a turn of chain should be taken around samsonpost or cleat without delay. It is unwise to hang on to the mooring and wait for the boat to steady before you belay. If she is carrying too much way or falls off, you may have more weight than you can handle, and have to let go; a weak pennant might part. *Never* wind a pennant round wrist or arm to get a purchase. It is inviting injury. Once the boat has steadied down, the quick belay may be cast off and the mooring properly secured.

It is not recommended to lie to rope or wire for any length of stay. Chafe makes short work of rope unless it is well parcelled (wrapped with canvas or leather), but even the parcelling itself can chafe through or come adrift. Wire rope looks deceptively tough but, once it begins to fray, can part abruptly. Chain is the correct answer, and even that needs attention. Bow rollers and leads should be well rounded off, as sharp edges will abrade galvanising and eventually wear through chain. Ideally, any bow lead should be closed with a drop-nose pin or similar device; a chain which jumps out of its lead can chew up caprail and topsides very quickly if the motion is at all lively.

Chain should be belayed with care. It can jam badly, which not only makes it difficult to release but can distort and weaken it. Figures of eight and jamming turns should not be used with chain; it can be taken several times around a large cleat and then belayed to a stout back-up point such as the foot of the mast. A samsonpost is preferred to a cleat. The best method of belay is shown in Fig 7. This is secure and simple to release. It is also

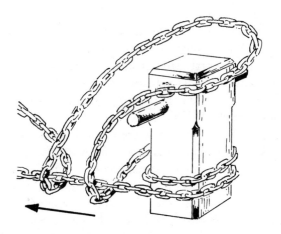

Fig 7 How to belay chain. The arrow shows the load

excellent to use with rope warps, when the end should be taken under the standing part a second time and another bight passed over the post in the reverse direction.

GRP boats are seldom found with a samsonpost, and any mooring cleats should be bolted through the deck to a large backing plate in order to spread the load. Mock samsonposts only bolted through deck are to be found, but they do not extend down to the keel. Unless backed by a massive plate these may pull away if heavily stressed, as the pull exerted on them is not close to and parallel with the deck.

Fig 8 shows a useful device for a permanent mooring, consisting of a large bollard strop of nylon which is shackled into the end of the chain. It lies along the deck, which it does not scuff or cover with rust stains, and drops snugly over the post or cleat to which it has been tailored. Only enough chain is taken aboard to lie over the stemhead against chafe, and the strop can be sized accordingly. It is quite feasible simply to shackle the end of a chain back on itself to form a similar bight, but this is unkind to deck surfaces, and also noisy.

Singlehanded problems
Mooring up is always a chore and can be slightly hazardous for a lone hand. To get smartly forward and lift a buoy in motion can be difficult; the craft can fall off and you should rightly attach your harness, which takes valuable seconds. The whole business can be undertaken from the security of the cockpit if advance preparation is made. On the market are spring-loaded crooks with a tongue that closes them once the crook has been pulled away from its shaft, on which it fits in a slide. A length of stout line is measured to lead from the samsonpost over the bow lead and back to the cockpit outside all. It is permanently shackled into the detachable crook and the other end is equipped with a soft eye to drop over the post. Arriving at the buoy, you casually lean out of the cockpit, sweep under the buoy and pull. The crook traps the pennant and the boat is secured. When everything has steadied, you stroll forward and secure at leisure. Make sure that your pennant is sound, and beware of picking up the mooring with too much way on; when the boat reaches the end of

the artificially lengthened scope, she will snub round and gybe.

Selecting a casual mooring
Where choice exists, it pays to sail around and be observant before deciding on an unfamiliar mooring. Some buoys will be marked with the name and holding capacity of the tackle; these indicate

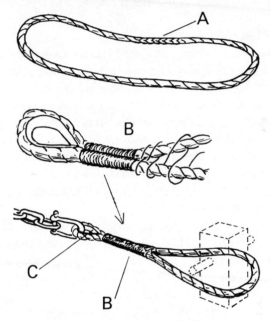

Fig 8   Permanent mooring strop
A Short splice
B Racking and seizing
C Thimble

a careful owner and will likely be well found. Others will have a derelict air with masses of weed trailing down below. Shun them. In addition to probable unreliability they will fetch weed, mud and rust aboard you and weigh a ton.

It is unwise for a deep keel boat to moor among those of shallow draught, and vice versa. The former will lie into the stream and the latter into wind, in addition to which they are prone to sheer about.

Any mooring should be taken with an eye to getting away in a hurry, perhaps in the dark. It may be preferable to accept a longer pull ashore than be seriously hemmed in by obstructions and other craft. Prevailing conditions of wind and water should be ascertained—local advice is to be had for the asking and may dictate the advisability of moving from the initially chosen spot.

Varieties of mooring
Simple swinging moorings as described are easy to handle, but other types exist and may cause bother on first encounter. Fore and aft moorings are used where swinging room is limited, and lines have to be taken fore and aft to pairs of buoys or pairs of piles. In some cases a single buoy is lifted to disclose a pennant leading to one chain forward and another aft; one has to deal with miles of slimy rope in getting them. In many continental harbours craft lie to anchor forward with a stern line to the quay, calling for the use of a gangplank or vaulting pole. Varieties on the theme are manifold.

A mooring pile usually has an upright bar upon which slides a metal ring. Warps should be made fast to the ring and not to the bar or pile. If other craft are already tied up, it is simple to fetch the ring, but if not, it may have to be lifted from the bottom of the bar. A light lifting chain should be there for the purpose, but these are often adrift and a boathook has to be used.

With pair mooring, a normal upstream approach will bring your bows alongside the forward pile for belaying the head line. This should be done with a round turn and two halfhitches or a fisherman's bend (see Figs 22–3). Do not use clove or other jamming hitches, as they will pull up solid under strain. It is inadvisable to use a warp doubled through the ring and taken back aboard; although easy to slip, it will chafe badly, as will a bowline used for making fast. With the headline secured, you can perhaps drop back to the aft pile to make fast the sternline, but if there is insufficient scope, it can be taken out in the tender. The boat should be positioned midway between the piles or buoys without so much slack that she will snub hard on change of stream or in adverse conditions.

Pile moorings in popular harbours usually hold a press of visiting boats. Large fenders are needed and you should take care to tie up alongside a boat with compatible freeboard. Ensure that shrouds and crosstrees do not get entangled and damaged. Lines taken to an inside boat are breastropes only, and each vessel should take out fore and aft lines. The tender can be handed along neighbours' warps already taken out. Springs taken to adjoining boats will prevent fore and aft surging, with danger to abutting rigging.

With the arrival and departure of others, your boat will get nearer and nearer to the centre of a trot or to the quayside, entailing adjustment of warps for scope. Minor damage is commonplace in trots, and I would always seek the alternative of a convenient anchorage.

An approach under sail to an occupied trot is unlikely to be greeted with acclamation, and sailing up to a quay or jetty needs careful anticipation. With an onshore wind, boom, rigging and sails can be damaged and the boat blown against the wall. Downstream of boats lying alongside there will be eddies, which are a trap for the unwary. With wind off the quay, a line has to be got ashore and secured smartly to avoid an ignominious retreat into the offing. It is more sensible to use your motor, but with all sail ready to rehoist if necessary. An anchor should be readied to trip if the engine stalls, resulting in a lack of steerage way in confined quarters. Warps should be ready to heave, hand out or take ashore. They should be coiled to run clear, with the inboard end taken through a fairlead and belayed in advance.

Warps
Warps are important and expensive items. They should be long enough, strong enough and of the right material. It is uncono-

mical and wasteful of stowage space to carry too many. The basic requirements could be two 75ft head and stern lines, two 40ft springs and two lighter 20ft breastropes.

As so much depends on their integrity, it is false economy to buy them undersized or of inferior stuff: 1½in nylon or terylene is the minimum acceptable for a 5-tonner and 2in would be better if it can be afforded. It is not so much the breaking strain that matters as the ability to stand up to hard usage. If properly looked after, synthetic warps will last a long time, and it is better, therefore, to spend more at the outset than to have something not fully suitable. Nylon and terylene are excellent, nylon's springiness making it perhaps the better choice, but other materials may be suspect. Some are susceptible to chafe and those that float are vulnerable to damage from propellers. They are also a confounded nuisance, and many harbours forbid their use.

In common with all lines, warps should be coiled for stowing, and the neatest method is to use the standard Admiralty hitch shown in Fig 9. Such a coil is easily undone and then lies ready to run out clear. The tail can be bighted with a bowline for hanging up. Nothing is more seamanlike and handy than a neat array of coils hung on labelled pegs.

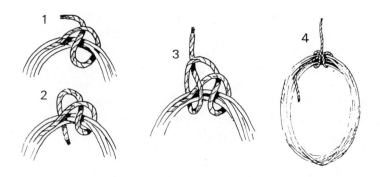

Fig 9 Hitching a coil of rope. Round, under and through (1); down and under (2); over and under (3); and pull and stow (4)

Belaying warps
The best belay around a samsonpost is shown in Fig 7. Figures of eight put around a cleat should always start with a round turn, and if two full figures of eight are put on top of it, there is no need to finish off with a reverse turn or other jam, as commonly seen. *A correctly selected and tied knot or hitch will hold without elaboration; it is either wrongly made up or wrongly chosen if it does not.* When belaying a warp inboard in advance, make sure that the first turn is taken from the outboard end, or the belay will jam under strain and be difficult to case off.

Ashore one usually belays to some sort of bollard or ring. It is convenient to drop a soft eye over a bollard. It should be about

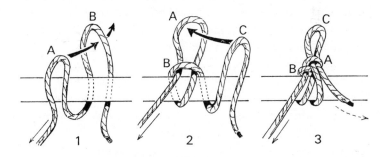

Fig 10 The highwayman's cutaway. Take bights A and B (1); pass bight A through bight B, and take bight C (2); and pass bight C through bight A and tighten (3). The lower arrows indicate load and the broken arrow the pull to release

3ft long and is better spliced in than made up with a bowline, which reduces the strength of the line. This eye should be led *up* through others lying on the bollard so that any one of them can be cast off independently. Similarly a warp should be led up through a ring before it is made fast with a round turn and two halfhitches or a fisherman's bend; the existence of a spliced eye will not interfere with this. Open-ended warps should be finished off with whippings—backsplicing is a lazy way to end a rope and will cause it to jam in rings and under thumbcleats.

It is common practice to lead a warp through a ring or round a bollard and secure both ends inboard ready to slip on getting away. This is convenient, especially when shorthanded, but it is better to use an alternative device which has no likelihood of jamming in ring or round bollard. The hitch illustrated (Fig 10) is not rendered bodily around ring or bollard; if carefully made, it works infallibly, and a sharp tug on the free end brings everything clear. It rejoices in the grand name of 'The highwayman's cutaway'.

GETTING UNDER WAY

On casting off, a helmsman has two objectives—to get his boat under complete command without delay and to have a plan of action for emergency. At such a time he will find it essential to understand the effects of natural forces on his boat, helpful or otherwise.

When a boat slips a free-swinging mooring she can be expected to gather sternway, the exact direction being governed by conditions of wind and water, and has then to be turned so as to sail ahead. Astern steering offers some slight difficulties to the inexperienced, and the following hints will give confidence:

1. Forget about port and starboard for the moment;
2. Face aft;
3. Move the tiller to your *left*; the stern of the boat will move to the *right*; and vice versa;
4. Move the *top* of a wheel in the direction you wish the stern to move; it will follow.

Just as steering movements come naturally when you face ahead, so going astern seems equally natural providing you face the direction of motion. Most confusion arises through trying to steer when facing forward and looking over your shoulder.

Sailing out astern

Fig 11 explains how to make a successful sternboard out of a tight situation. A foresail is raised and sheeted in hard, whereupon

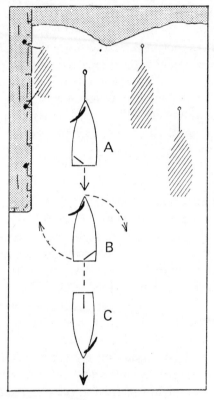

Fig 11 Making a sternboard

A Jib backed to port, tiller over to port
B Jib still backed, tiller over to starboard
C Tiller amidships, jib filling

the boat will range about as the sail backs and fills. As it comes up to full aback (ie with the wind coming in over the side on which the sail is sheeted), slip your mooring and hold the tiller over just enough to windward to cancel out the tendency of the bows to pay off along the arc in B. The boat will sail straight astern and, when in the clear, can be rotated rapidly as you reverse the tiller, so that the waterflow augments the pressure of wind on the head-sail instead of balancing it. The sail will fill if you then check the sheet, and the boat can be sailed on to a position where it is possible to round up and raise the main at ease.

It is advisable not to raise the mainsail initially because, although the boat might make a satisfactory sternboard, the main-sheet will have to be left free and the boom will be a bit of a nuisance. If the sail were at all hardened in, the boat would try to make headway while still moored and start to run off at an angle when slipped. Also, after turning end for end, she might gather unwanted speed.

Slipping a quay
You have to plan how to leave any quay or jetty along which a stream is flowing. It can flow from ahead or astern as you lie tied up, and the wind can be roughly assessed as ahead, astern, onshore or offshore, which gives eight different combinations of effects. Onshore breezes usually preclude sailing away—the use of warps in this situation is discussed later. Added to whichever of the six remaining combinations exists must be the direction in which you want to head after slipping. On this last point rests the decision as to what sail to set beforehand.

To run downstream under full sail in a crowded harbour would not be as prudent as leaving under foresail only. To beat out against a stream might call for full plain sail and a smart hand on the sheets. With good planning there should be little difficulty, but lack of forethought can cause things to become a little fraught.

Fig 12 shows four of the many situations to be met with, and you will have to learn through experience and practice how best to handle your own boat in similar circumstances. Two points are worth mentioning:

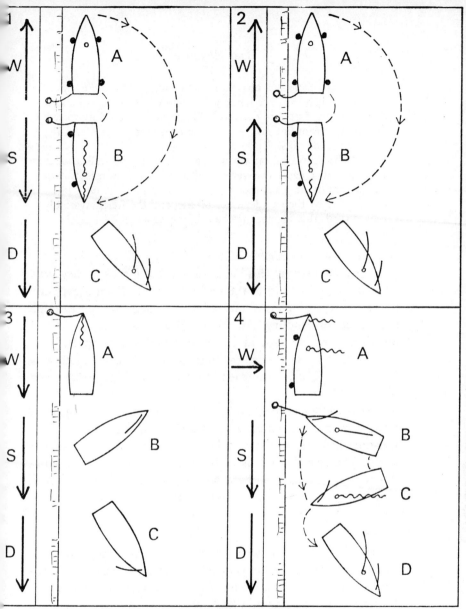

Fig 12 Ways of slipping a quayside. The arrows indicate direction of
wind, stream and intended departure

    1 A No sail set, set fenders outboard, and warp round into wind
       B Raise main and jib, cast off forward
       C Sheet both sails hard in, push bows off, cast off smartly aft
    2 A Warp round into wind (don't forget extra fenders)
       B Raise main and jib, let go aft
       C Let go forward, push bows off then stern, sheet in main and jib
    3 A Raise jib, let go aft
       B Let go forward, sheet jib to starboard, push nose off
       C Set out under jib
    4 A Raise main and jib, let go aft, sheet in main
       B She will then lie like this
       C Back jib, let go forward, make sternboard
       D Away you go

1. With free sheets a boat will tend to align itself to the water-flow, but when they are hardened in she will start to sail ahead and then round up into the wind. This makes it necessary to cast off the upstream line *last*, so that the boat points away from the quay when the sails fill;

2. If she moves off on a course parallel with the wall, rudder movement will cause the stern to swing inwards towards it, with the possibility of grazing or collision. Boats pivot about a point determined by their underwater profile, and the stern invariably moves through a greater arc than do the bows.

Auxiliary motors—use and failures

Use of an auxiliary is sensible in tight conditions, but they have been known to fail just at the critical moment. Even if perfectly reliable and scrupulously maintained a motor can fail through mishap or mishandling. An unopened exhaust cock, a scrap of polythene drifting around the water intake, a warp let drift around the propeller—many such things will bring the motor to a sudden stop. If it is insufficiently warmed up, it may stall when put under load.

It is therefore prudent to have sail either hoisted or ready to raise at immediate notice. As slides can jam and halyards foul, it can do little harm to have a heaving line ready and an anchor a'trip. You may think this to be taking prudence to the limit, but if streams run at all hard and the breeze is strong, a small snag can snowball into near disaster in no time at all.

Warping

If pinned against a wall without a motor, you will find that warps and kedges can be used to gain clear space for raising sail. Warps can be used to shift a boat along a quayside, turn her end for end, transfer from one side of a harbour to the other and so on. No great effort is needed to move a boat as long as a steady continuous strain is exerted.

A warp can be taken out in a tender, say from one wall to another or from the quay out to a buoy. It is pointless to ferry out the end of a warp coiled aboard the boat. It should be carefully faked down to run clear over the sternsheets of the tender, and this calls for two crew. A light line may be taken out initially to bring out the heavier warp. If short warps have to be joined, the knot to use is the carrick bend, which is utterly secure and simple to take out, as it does not jam under load; other methods of joining may do so. If there are soft eyes in the warps, they can be joined by thoroughfooting, as illustrated in Fig 13.

Fig 13 Joining warps

A Carrick bend. Lead as shown. Both short ends must be on same side
B Thoroughfooting warps

Kedging off

A warp and kedge (anchor) can be rowed out in order to move a boat to a desired position. A kedge is customarily used to haul a boat out of a lee position to where sail can be made or the bower anchor laid. It may be necessary to kedge off in stages: the boat is taken out to the kedge, the bower laid, kedge lifted and taken further out—and the process can be repeated as often as required.

An anchor in a tender is heavy and unhandy. It should be slipped over the transom of a hard dinghy, *never* over the side. If possible it should be lashed outboard of the transom, and prepared ready to drop while the tender is still moored up fore and aft to the boat. Secure the kedge to a thwart with a spare piece of line; use a sliphitch such as the highwayman's cutaway for ease of release. The kedge should be lowered carefully and not let drop, in case coils of warp ensnare unwary feet.

Tenders

Great care must be taken when rowing out a kedge and, indeed, at other times when using a tender. All crew should wear personal buoyancy as a routine and the tender should be sufficiently buoyant to support itself and its crew in the event of capsizing. You would be wise to check this at leisure and, if needs be, improve buoyancy by lashing inflatable bags fore and aft under thwarts after the fashion of racing dinghies. More people are lost from tenders and other small craft, often close inshore or even in harbour, than ever drown from yachts at sea. Never overlook the fact that *small boats are potentially dangerous*.

When alongside loading and unloading crew or gear, a tender should be made fast fore *and* aft to the parent boat. If only held by a single painter, it can too easily skate away and foothold be lost.

Inflatables are not easy to row, due to their lack of grip on the water, and are intractable in bad conditions, which makes the use of an outboard inescapable. Warps and kedges can then be let down over the side to avoid fouling the propeller—inflatables are inherently more stable than hard tenders, but they *can* be capsized. Once again personal buoyancy is needed, and a line should be fitted all round the outside of an inflatable for the crew to hold on to if it turns over. The preferable type of inflatable has sponsons which project aft of the outboard mounting. Where the motor hangs out over a blunt transom and the crew sits well aft to handle it, a sudden gust can cause the tender to flip over backwards, to the embarrassment of its crew.

Towing

A boat can be towed along with her tender if needs be, and in this case use of an outboard saves much effort. It is best to lash the tender alongside and use the boat's tiller to steer the tandem. It is pointless to try to tow from the bows with an inflatable, as it has virtually no directional stability.

OARS, SWEEPS AND SCULLS

A sweep is an oversized oar and a pair of them can be used successfully to propel quite large boats, one resting over each gunwale in a rowlock or over a tholepin. Small cruisers can be rowed from the cockpit, whereas larger craft may call for one man per sweep toiling on deck. They face fore or aft, as suits the circumstances, and can walk to and fro along any deck which is clear enough. Such activity is practised by inshore fishermen in many parts of the world. A type of sweep that is difficult to lose overboard is illustrated (Fig 14). Used by crabbers, who have to release their oars frequently to tend their pot lines, these sweeps look clumsy but are in fact easy and effective to use.

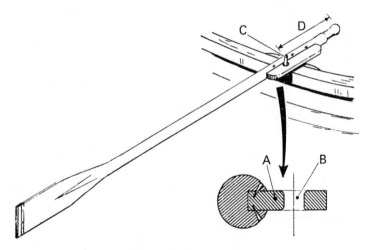

Fig 14 Potboat sweep

A Block of wood securely fastened into slot in oar's shaft
B Hole through block fits loosely over tholepin
C Wood or metal tholepin set into gunwale
D Normal distance from boat's centreline to gunwale

Sweeps are awkward items to stow but can be lashed along a guardrail, or upright against a shroud.

Sculling
This is a good way of propelling a small boat and can be em-

ployed on much larger craft to excellent effect. The sculling oar is placed in a notch carved out of the top of the transom, which is rounded at the bottom to accept the loom of the oar and deep enough to prevent it slipping out when in use. It should be about one and a half times as deep as the diameter of the loom. It is usually central in the transom, but this is not essential, and in a boat with a transom-hung rudder the notch can be offset without detriment. Fig 15 shows the placement of a sculling oar and the method of using it.

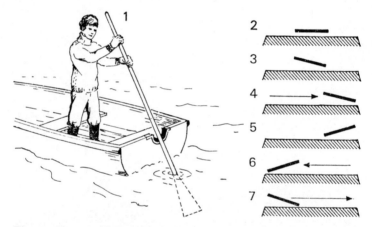

Fig 15 How to scull. Stand facing aft, and immerse blade 1ft (1); grasp shaft with hands opposing, wrists straightened (2); use wrists to incline blade (3); push with right hand and pull with left (4); rotate wrists to reverse inclination of blade (5); push with left hand, pull with right (6); rotate blade again, and so on (7). The blade should be kept as near to the angle of transom as is shown. The force required to maintain this angle (about 60°) will be the force transmitted to the blade

It is used more like a fish's tail or propeller than as a fulcrum for leverage, as in rowing. The knack lies in the correct positioning of the wrists, which must be held below the level of the loom and not out to the side. The trunk will sway rhythmically from side to side and the top of the loom describe a sort of figure eight.

The art takes a little mastering, like riding a bicycle, and should be tackled to start with by standing up and facing aft. By watching your wake you can ultimately hope to achieve a straight course, but do not forget to glance regularly in the direction of travel. A small boat will roll gently to compensate for the sculler's movements, and it might be better to learn from the security of a cockpit. Not only will this prevent unpremeditated immersion but bring the realisation that quite large craft can be propelled in this way. Of course, the larger the boat the slower and more stately the progress!

Paddling
In emergency almost anything long and rigid can be used to paddle a boat along—boathooks, floorboards and so on—but it is prudent to carry at least one oar on every boat. This applies to motorboats, where such a sensible precaution is often overlooked.

ELEMENTS OF TROUBLEFREE HANDLING
As a young man inclined to gadgetry I was sternly told to eschew such nonsense and stick to the *kiss* principle—keep it simple, stupid. This was many years ago, but the advice is even more relevant today when gadgets and gimmicks abound. Efficient gear and correct routines for using it contribute greatly to trouble-free handling. Deck gear should in essence be stout, simple, easy to handle under all conditions, and foolproof; and should fail safe if it fails at all.

One has to build up an attitude of mind which argues that there is a right and proper way of performing every task—the correct selection and impeccable making of the knot, bend or hitch for the job in hand; a routine sequence of reducing and changing sails; gradual preparation for the anticipated change in weather, good or bad; and so on. In short, the development of drills to deal with all contingencies to be met with afloat. It does not do to become inflexible in outlook, of course, and routines may have to be varied or even abandoned at times, although this will seldom happen to reliable ones.

Habits are readily formed, for good or bad, and it is best to start out right. There is no single or perfect way of doing anything, and every sailor has his own ideas and methods. Time spent crewing for old salts gives opportunity to observe, select and reject various ways of tackling problems before you crystallise your own habits.

Mainsails

A mainsail can be pulled out of shape, with resulting loss of looks and efficiency, by continual incorrect hoisting. The weight of a boom, which may be considerable, should be taken on a crutch or topping lift to relieve the leech from stretch until the sail is fully up. A lesser known reason for distortion is illustrated in Fig 16.

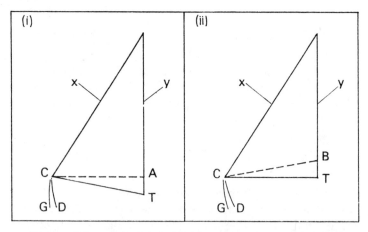

Fig 16　Distortion of mainsail. T=tack, x=leech and y=luff

In Fig 16(i) the tack of the sail is less than a rightangle and the distance AC is less than the foot CT. When the halyard is checked, the weight of the boom is taken by the sail. The clew C should rightly follow the path CD but is constrained to follow the arc CG, which it can only do by being stretched out of shape.

In Fig 16(ii) the tack is a rightangle (or more) but the luffrope slides are retained in the track at point B. There will be stretching along the line CB, which can be prevented if the retainer is opened and a slide or two released from the track.

In both cases, if a crutch or lift is used to stop the clew dropping below point C, no problem will arise.

Mainsheet

Alloy booms will not flex unduly, no matter at what point along them the pull of the mainsheet is exerted, so that positioning of the mainsheet block is a mátter of choice. It is often more convenient to mount it partway along than at boom end, as traditionally and almost invariably with wooden spars.

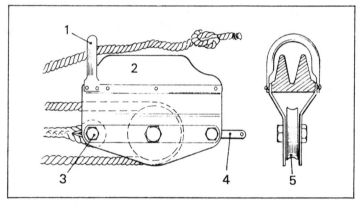

Fig 17　Mainsheet block. Fairlead (1), clamcleat (2), becket (3), slide fitting (4), and sheave (5)

Sheets leading from the end of a boom can be embarrassing in a small cockpit and possibly hazardous to crew, as in the case of an involuntary gybe. If wholly forward of crew terrain, they will be more acceptable, and can often be taken to a block running in a track mounted on the bridgedeck or coachroof. This shortens the fulcrum for leverage and the sheet may have to reeve through a greater purchase. Reefing complications caused by midboom sheeting are discussed later in this chapter.

The smaller the boat the greater the need for a mainsheet belay which can be easily released but is at the same time secure. I have used the type of block shown in Fig 17 for years and found it most satisfactory. It is easy to make, but there seems to be no similar commercial model available. It is obviously necessary to use blocks which can be derigged; those where the sheaves are held in by riveted pins are useless.

Foresails

These sails are best hanked on a stay. If set flying, ie tautened on their own luff wire unsupported, they are hard to handle in a breeze and their luffs cannot be made taut enough for windward work. Strong piston hanks of suitable metal should be fitted, for a stainless steel forestay will soon chew through soft stuff. Hanks should be examined frequently for wear, distortion and weakened piston springs. The piston slide needs frequent but sparing lubrication, or else too much oil will get on to the sails.

A purchase of some sort is essential to achieve a taut luff, and choice abounds between winches, tail tackles, tack downhauls and so on. In using them attention must be given to the height of the tack of the foresail above deck, as this governs the setting of the sheet lead aft. If a halyard purchase is used, each sail should be permanently fitted with a correctly sized wire strop at the tack. Examples of purchases are given in Fig 18.

A tack downhaul is a useful means of getting beef into a luff as the pull can be made upwards, enabling the thigh muscles to be brought into use. One can also get an upward pull if a halyard purchase is finished as shown in Fig 18(A). When using a tack downhaul, care must be taken to hoist the head of the sail to the same point each time so that the height of the tack above deck does not vary. This means that each sail will have to be hoisted to an individual height depending on the length of its luff. Try the following expedient.

The halyard is made up with a cut splice for each headsail carried. These fit snugly over a convenient half-cleat on the mast and are measured so that when the downhaul has been swigged

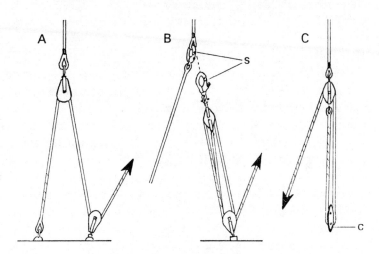

Fig 18 Examples of purchases

A 2:1 purchase. Rope halyard led through single block spliced into end of wire halyard, shackled to deck and led through lazy block for upward pull

B Rope tail snapshackled (s) into eye at end of wire halyard. When nearing eye of hoist, a tackle is snapped into eye for final tensioning—tail can then be removed and stowed. Very neat method

C Snatch block spliced into end of wire halyard and rope tail spliced to lower end of block. For final tensioning, rope is led round cleat (c) and through snatch block for purchase (3:1), and is then belayed on cleat

up the tack of each sail will be correctly positioned. A mark corresponding to each sail is made on the sheet lead tracks, or if fixed leads are used, they can be correctly stationed.

The cost of a small foresail can often be saved if a larger one is fitted for reefing, which was common practice in working boats. A line of reefpoints can be sewn in, as described a little later; this should be parallel with the foot of the sail.

Roller furling gear is not suitable for reefing purposes, as the head of the sail will pull out, with inefficient setting and possible damage. Patent roller reefing gear for foresails is coming on the market, but, as this means rotating joints in the forestay, they may not stand up to offshore conditions. Failure could cost you your mast. Of course, time may prove their suitability, and a means of safely and swiftly reefing a foresail is much to be desired.

Halyards

Halyards can be of rope, wire or rope-tailed wire, according to the demands of a boat. Wire stretches less, offers less windage and is stronger per diameter than rope. It is less tractable to handle and, if not tailed with rope, must be kept on a self-stowing winch. Prestretched terylene halyards are excellent for smaller boats, and their elongation at full load, which muscle power will seldom impose, is not more than about 3 per cent. Such stuff is quieter, easier to stow and splice, and more comfortable to handle than wire. Rope halyards seldom jam in their sheaves, which is not uncommon with wire, as their diameter is greater than the clearance between sheave and its housing. They can be used over an open winch or led through a purchase. Plaited rope may be found less satisfactory than laid, for foresail halyards particularly, both to handle and to run out clear. A small diameter halyard may be quite strong enough, but hard on the hands, in which case it is a simple matter to splice on a tail of greater diameter for ease of handling.

Sheaves

It is imperative that a sheave of the right size, shape of groove and hardness should be used at the masthead for wire halyards. One that jumps its sheave may jam in the housing and present a hazard; it is not simple to get aloft to clear such a jam at sea, and it may be most urgent to lower sail at the time. If rope halyards are ever replaced by wire, it is essential to change sheaves accordingly, or trouble will sooner or later be inevitable.

Sheets

Wire sheets are unlikely to be found on small cruisers, but the purchase of rope requires thought. Synthetics are expensive and durable, so a sheet should be chosen with care. Sheets which render through a purchase should run easily and smoothly. They should be comfortable to the hand which often means a larger size than needed for strength alone. Plaited rope is suitable for mainsheets, and comes in many varieties designed expressly for the purpose; they should be bought for softness and ease of grasp. A sheet should not be excessively long, as bights cluttering a cockpit are a nuisance, but a little extra should be bought on grounds of economy. A sheet should be turned end for end periodically to minimise chafe at blocks and cleats. When chafe, or stretch, becomes noticeable, a few inches taken off the out-board end of a mainsheet will permit fresh surfaces to feed through points of chafe.

Similar considerations of chafe and stretch apply to foresail sheets, but these are subjected to a much harder life. They wear at fairleads, where lengths of them feed round a winch, and where they rub against shrouds and rigging, and they are heavily stressed. Again, turn them end for end and fit such anti-chafe gear as shroud rollers and swivelling blocks for fairleads rather than bullseyes. Cam cleats murder jibsheets and clam cleats are preferred, although if a sheet is likely to be subjected to fluctuating loads, or surging and flogging, the most secure belay is the traditional horn pattern.

It is important to secure the sheet properly to the clew cringle of a foresail. Snapshackles can unsnap themselves or get caught in rigging when sheets are checked. Screwpin shackles are fiddly and take time to secure when changing sail; they can occasionally unscrew, and a lost and flailing foresail is a thing to be avoided at all costs. The Scandinavian type illustrated (Fig 19) can be secured with the fingers and is stronger for its weight than most other types.

Whatever shackle is used, you will usually find it entered into an eye seized into the middle of a double-ended sheet, and this is subjected to great wear and tear as it chafes on and catches in rigging. Many an otherwise serviceable sheet has had to be discarded as a result. If a few extra inches are available, the worn

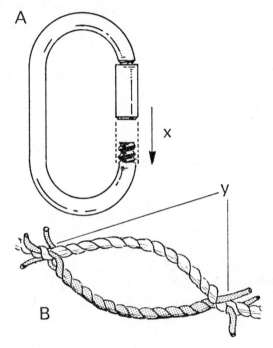

Fig 19 Jib sheet gear

A Scandinavian type—screws down (x)
B Repair with a cut splice and ends spliced in (y)

eye can be cut out and the rope repaired with a cut splice; a round thimble seized into this will help prevent further wear.

Shackles can be done away with altogether and sheets made to last much longer if each sail is fitted with a short rope pendant spliced into the clew. This is fastened into the eye of the sheet with a sheet bend—the knot designed for the purpose. It can be undone readily if the top bight is pushed over the standing part with finger and thumb.

Control of sheets and halyards

It is unseamanlike to lose control of either end of a sheet or halyard. Whenever the fall of a rope is taken through a block or other lead, it should be stoppered with a thumbknot or figure of eight knot. The lower block of any purchase close to the deck should be of the swivelling type and shackled to a deckeye.

The hoist end of any halyard needs control to prevent it getting adrift and streaming out from the masthead, a common sight. This is not so likely to occur with a main halyard, as it is seldom removed from the headboard while at sea, but foresail halyards need attention. They can be held close to the forestay if a pin shackle is passed through the eye and taken around the stay; the pin should be inside the thimble and not run up and down the stay, or it may come adrift. This fitment has the added advantage of holding the head of the sail close to the stay, when it will set better.

When changing foresails, the hoist end of the halyard coming out of use can be secured conveniently to a short shockcord permanently secured to the pulpit or thereabouts.

Winches

Any winch handle not secured inboard with a lanyard will go overboard sooner or later. Riding turns on a winch are dangerous; they can jam solid and make it impossible to let go the sheet short of cutting it away. It helps to prevent riding turns if the sheet is led correctly on to the barrel, and too many turns are not put around it. One turn will allow a sail to be sheeted in to the point where one more is needed before applying the handle. In strong breezes a third turn may be used to prevent slip, but this should be the lot. To wind on more than one turn when a sheet is slack is asking for trouble.

Sheet leads will end at different points on the deck, according to the sail in use, and not all of these will render fairly to the winch barrel. It is best to site a swivelling block in the optimum position and take all sheets finally through this.

Sheet leads

The termination at deck level of a sheet depends on the characteristics of the sail in use. It is of advantage to be able to vary the lead of a sheet somewhat in different strengths of breeze, and for this reason preferable to use an adjustable block in a track than a static deckeye upon which a block is swivelled. Bullseyes and such leads cause friction when a sheet renders through them under load, and may cause synthetic rope to glaze through over-heating. If any sort of static lead is used instead of block and track, it means that multiple sheets have to be kept led to allow for sail changes, and this causes snarls. If only one sheet is used, it has to be taken out and re-led each time the headsail is changed.

Topping lifts

These are sometimes omitted from a boat's tally but are really an essential adjunct to making sail and to reefing. They can be used as an emergency standby for a parted halyard. Their disadvantage is that they must be given slack when sail is drawing, and then they whip about and rub the leech, with resultant chafe and broken stitching. Light line will serve as well and be kinder than small wire. If a topping lift ends in a snapshackle, once sail is set it can be detached from the boom and snapped into a small ring seized on to a backstay. If this is sensibly positioned, there will be no need to adjust the lift for length before or after attaching it to the boom. Alternatively the lift can be detached from the boom and belayed back about the foot of the mast. In any case it calls for a routine to ensure that it is clipped back on to the boom before the main halyard is ever checked.

Gallows

A gallows into which a heavy boom can be steered and secured is useful for reefing and stowing, but such bulky equipment is not suitable for a small boat. Detachable boom crutches are often seen but they are of dubious advantage, as they either get bent or lost overboard. Their place can be taken by a short wire pendant seized on to a backstay which ends in a snapshackle that can clip into an eye on the end of the boom. If high enough, it will keep the boom stowed above head height when not sailing. It can be used for holding the boom when reefing, but in that case the mainsheet should be hardened in and impeccably belayed. A crewman may be using both hands and resting all his weight on the boom at such a time and must not be at risk.

Chafe

Chafing of sails and rope is a bugbear. Where a sail bears on rigging or spreaders, it will wear thin and stitching come adrift. Sheets are hauled past shrouds, through leads and blocks and round winches.

Aids can be devised to minimise chafe, but the baggywrinkle beloved of many looks out of place on a small boat and is not really very effective, anyway. Where a sail habitually bears against rigging, it can be reinforced with a patch, or patch on both sides. Soft pads—a sorbo ball cut and taped on, or a proprietary article —can be fitted to the ends of spreaders.

Shroud rollers are very effective, and should be thought about before eyes are made in the ends of the standing rigging, otherwise they will be difficult, if not impossible, to fit. Where rope runs through blocks, their cheeks should be rounded down if necessary and smoothly finished with fine wet and dry emerycloth. Stemhead rollers are often poorly made, with sharp edges that should similarly be rounded down and polished to cut down on chain wear.

Sails allowed to flog in a swell on a calm day will wear much more quickly than under sailing conditions, and should be lowered until the breeze is re-established. When a boat is brought up into any strength of breeze, the headsail should be handed as soon as possible and not allowed to flap and flail about.

The intelligent use of observation and attention to chafe and abrasion will save money and trouble, not only to the long-distance sailor but to every boatowner.

KNOTS

This word is commonly used to include bends and hitches, and it seems sensible to do so in these pages. A knot must be chosen to fit the purpose for which it is intended and, although there are many hundreds of them, the fewer and simpler the number you use the better.

The important thing is that you should train your fingers to make the essential knots infallibly in any conceivable circumstances, *without looking*. Equally vital is the ability to be able to release them easily and rapidly; delay can frequently be embarrassing and occasionally dangerous. Knots which might jam under load or let go in certain circumstances should be avoided, and this situation can be brought about by the incorrect selection of a knot.

Over-elaborate knots are certainly to be avoided, as it is so easy to make them incorrectly. A common failing is to embroider a simple knot under the impression that it will be more secure, but any knot correctly chosen and properly made up can be relied on to do its job. A round turn and two halfhitches for example, will serve just as well and be infinitely easier to undo than a quadruple and ten.

Figs 20–28 show the appearance, when made, of probably all the knots that are needed on a small boat. Readers are invited to start from scratch and sort things out for themselves. Everyone has his own way of handling line and, providing the knot turns out as depicted, it matters little how the thing was done. Constant practice is essential to keep your hand in.

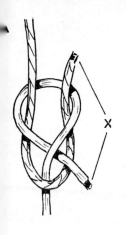
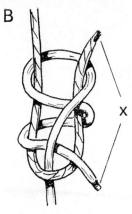

B

Fig 20 Sheet bend (A) and double sheet bend (B). Ensure that both short ends (x) are on the same side of the completed bend. Can be used for joining ropes of different diameters, and for bending a line on to a thimble. Make the bend with the smaller line. The double variety gives added security

Fig 21 Constrictor knot. This jams and holds better than a clove hitch, and is used for attaching a line or painter to a spar or post. Difficult to release

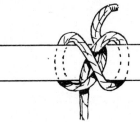

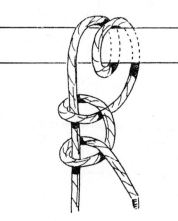

Fig 22 Round turn and two half-hitches. A general purpose knot for securing a line to spar, post or ring. Easy to release and does not jam

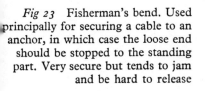

Fig 23 Fisherman's bend. Used principally for securing a cable to an anchor, in which case the loose end should be stopped to the standing part. Very secure but tends to jam and be hard to release

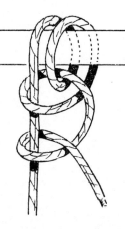

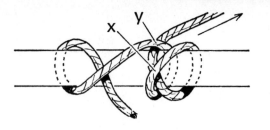

x y

Fig 24 Rolling hitch. For putting a load on a spar, shroud, cable an so on. Both turns must cross the standing part, ie at x and y. Very secure and simple to release. Arrow indicates load

Fig 25 Figure of eight knot. Used to stop the ends of lines passing through blocks, etc

Fig 26 Reef knot. Both short ends must be on the same side

Fig 27 Bowline. The best way of making a bight (loop, eye) in a rope for any purpose

1

2

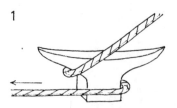

Fig 28 Cleat belay. First take a round turn (1), and follow on with figures of eight (2). Arrows indicate load

REEFING

Putting in and taking out reefs is part of the business of sailing, and every crewman should be able to reef efficiently without tiring himself. Two methods are to be found—roller reefing and points, or slab, reefing.

Roller reefing consists of wrapping the sail around the boom with the help of some form of mechanism. Many types are to be encountered, but they all rotate the boom in one way or another. This method is under some circumstances quicker and less tiring than points reefing but has the following disadvantages:

1. The outboard end of a circular boom droops because the luffrope winds up thick and the leech thin. Specially tapered booms will prevent this effect but are expensive and can only be got to order. Circular booms can be modified to approximate to a taper by the addition of lengthwise strips of wood or metal, known as whelps, which effectively do the same thing as a tapered boom but do not look so neat;

2. Unless the foot of the sail is kept taut by hauling on the leech during rolling, the sail gathers in unsightly and inefficient drapes. Two men, therefore, are needed to reef decently unless a simple device only suitable for very small sails is used. Here no winding mechanism is used, but the boom is shipped over a gooseneck which slips into a square hole in the endplate of the boom (Fig 29).

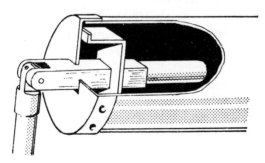

Fig 29 Simple roller reefing gear

55

By hauling aft on the boom the endplate slides into the round part of the pivot and can be rotated from the cockpit, while the leech is pulled out simultaneously. The gooseneck runs up and down in a track on the mast and, to begin reefing, is allowed to drop to the bottom of the track by checking the halyard. As the sail is rolled, the gooseneck rises to the top of the track, when another bite is taken. If the main halyard is led aft to the cockpit, such reefing is further simplified;

3. Despite care and lubrication, mechanical gear can fail or jam;

4. It should be routine to use a kicking strap for mainsail control, and it has to be unshipped when reefing for obvious reasons. Its point of attachment then becomes covered up by the rolled sail. A clawring can be used to attach it to the boom but this is hard on the cloth and the claw tends to become distorted. The best alternative is to use a strip of sailcloth as shown in Fig 30.

Points reefing

For points reefing a sail is fitted with patches in lines roughly level with the foot. Short lengths of line, known as points, are sewn into the centre of the patches and used for tidying away the bunt of sail left over after reefing. Alternatively, cringles are fitted in place of points and a lacing is passed through them for the same purpose. In larger craft booms are fitted with bee-blocks and sheaves for reefing, but in smaller craft these are not usually fitted. They are not essential and their absence will not be noticed, as will be seen shortly.

At luff and leech there are stout cringles at the end of each line of points. These are to enable the sail to be drawn down by means of pendants which can remain shipped during a passage or be reeved on each occasion of reefing. The routine for reefing is essentially simple, but the correct sequence must be followed if sails are to remain untorn:

1. Draw down the luff cringle and secure it with a lashing or hook about the region of the gooseneck;

2. Draw down the corresponding leech cringle. Lash it with the fall of the pendant so that the sail is both stretched tautly along and firmly held down against the top of the boom. In heavy

conditions it may be necessary to use a purchase to get this done, and it is for this reason that bee-blocks and sheaves are sometimes fitted;

3. Roll the surplus sail up neatly and secure it with points or lacings, as may be. Reefknots are used to secure points and this is their only purpose. A reefknot will capsize if one of the loose ends is pulled backwards, and the line will then pull free. Reef points are *NOT* stress points, their function being to tidy the sail away. They must never be tied in until both cringles are secure and always released before they are let go; if not a torn sail cannot be avoided.

As a preliminary to reefing, the boom must be secured in a gallows, crutch or otherwise prevented from movement. Routines for handling halyards, topping lifts and so on cannot be specified, as they will depend on the layout of a boat.

Fig 30 Kicking strap attachment. A strip of sailcloth with a strong eyelet sewn in. It should be long enough to be tucked into the rolls of sail round the boom, and taken around with the last two rolls. The kicking strap should then be shackled to the eyelet cringle

Unreefing calls for a precise reversal of the reefing routine.

Reefing and unreefing should really be carried out in stages of one line at a time, but in urgent circumstances it may be necessary to pull down a deep reef and omit the intervening ones.

When reefing by stages, take care not to muddle up the ends of points from different lines, or damage might ensue.

Two fittings can be used on small craft to assist reefing: one snaphook for each luff cringle fitted in the region of the gooseneck; and a self-jamming tackle of about 3:1 advantage for hauling out the foot of the sail. The latter can snap into an eye on the end of the boom and, when the foot has been hauled taut, the fall of the purchase is used to lash the cringle on to the top of the boom. This gear, pendants and everything else used for reefing should be stowed carefully in a bag, clearly marked and instantly available.

Reefing—general

If it gets difficult to reef during a blow, it helps to heave-to and reef in the lee of the backed foresail. If badly pressed, the mainsail can be lowered for reefing. Points reefing is then comparatively simple, but roller reefing can be muddlesome. It is wise to lie-to on the starboard tack, as this confers right of way, and for this reason the main halyard and the topping lift should belay on the starboard side of the mast.

Mainsails of cruising boats should ideally not have their luffropes running in a groove in the mast. In a breeze the sail can slide completely out of the mast if the halyard is mishandled, and will belly out and become unmanageable. The better fitting is a track or groove to contain slides fitted to the luffrope. The way sails are made makes modification of the headboard and its roping necessary if you wish to convert from one method to the other.

A groove in the boom is unobjectionable from the handling viewpoint, but points or lacings will then have to be taken right around the boom instead of being tucked neatly between boom and footrope. This may have to be accepted, and it is consoling to know that a grooved boom is slightly more efficient than one fitted with a track; it stops the formation of eddies around the bottom of the sail, which reduce efficiency.

It is worth emphasising that all sails normally rolled should be fitted with a deep line of points against failure of gear when reefing is imperative. The reef line should be placed so that the reefed sailed approximates to three-fifths of the total area. Lacing is preferred here, as the reef line will be used infrequently and points are a bit of a nuisance when rolling a sail.

RUNNING AGROUND

In shoal waters there is always a possibility of running aground, and no sailor should view this as other than a potentially serious matter. However, you may at times have to take a calculated risk, which is minimised if you are sure of your position, the tide is rising, the weather reasonable and the bottom acceptable.

The first concern should be for the weather. A grounding in fine conditions may be little more than a time-wasting setback, but in bad ones can be disastrous. Any sizeable swell or succession of seas can thump a boat repeatedly on the ground and damage the hull. With a falling tide the possibility of contact between ground and topsides could, in the extreme, cause total loss. Not only existing but future weather must be taken into account. In unsettled conditions 6hr is time enough for a light breeze to turn into a gale of wind.

The type of ground to be encountered is the next most important factor, and can range from rock through shale, shingle, clay, sand, mud and down to ooze. The composition of the seabed can change radically over a short distance, so that you should know your position to within close limits if the possibility of grounding exists. Bad visibility can extend the area of your probable position, which you must be able to estimate. Once this area widens to take in hazards, it is wise to alter course, slow down, anchor or take other action to keep out of trouble.

It helps to know the profile of the ground in your vicinity, which could be gently or steeply shoaling, a ledge, a middle ground that might make it easier to go ahead than astern when getting off, and so on. Try to visualise the ground beneath your keel and consult the chart for enlightenment. As soft ground is liable to constant change in depth and shape, little reliance can be placed on chart soundings in such an area, and confirmation of depth of water has to be made with echo sounder, leadline, pole, oar, boathook or the like. It pays to poke about as widely as possible, and the tender can be used to widen the area of search. An armed lead will fetch up a sample of the bottom for examination, but a bucket can be dragged along for the same purpose in shoal water.

Much depends on hull shape. A bilgekeeler is a better proposition than a finkeeler for taking the ground and will remain more or less on an even keel unless it drops into a hole or comes to rest on a protrusion. Finkeelers will lie over until one side of the hull rests on the ground. It is critical to decide which side she should lie on once you realise that she is *sewed*, and to take urgent steps to ensure that she does. (Sewed: pronounced 'sued'. Grounded until the following tide lifts you off.) Worse than sewing is beneaping—going aground at the top of a tide when succeeding tides are taking off (becoming lower and lower at high water). In these circumstances you will not have enough water to float you off until the corresponding time in the next tidal cycle. For example, if you go aground at high water halfway between spring and neap tides, the next floatable tide may well be halfway between neaps and springs on the next round, a lapse of a week or more. Beneaping is to be avoided; cases have occurred of boats being written off because bad weather intervened before they could be refloated. To go aground at the top of high springs could be a very dreary matter.

Providing that you do not drive on senselessly hard, on a rising tide there is really not more to do than lay out a kedge to prevent lifting and drifting further onshore as the water deepens. With a falling tide you must try to get afloat before you are *sewed*. It is more difficult to effect a quick recovery when the bottom slopes gently than when it is steep, as for each inch the water drops the farther you get from deeper water. Aids to quick refloating are wind and sails; motor; kedge, warps and tender; crew armed with poles, boathooks, oars or the like.

The possibility of being able to sail off a lee shore is not high and, as wind in the sails will drive you harder on, it may be urgent to lower them at once. If time is really pressing, they can just be let fly, but with a quartering wind there is no alternative but to lower them. At the first whisper of an anticipated touch you might be able to get the boat's head around enough to get the foresail aback, but this depends on which point of the keel has grounded. Folkboat keels typify those which slope gently aft and permit the heel to be in contact while the toe is still clear, but it may be only seconds before continued driving grounds the whole length of it. Haste is essential and the crew should come aft to raise the bows as much as possible. Other types of keel formation may dictate weight in the bows to clear the keel and get the boat off again.

It should be fairly easy to sail off a windward shore if you are only lightly grounded. Crew weight can be used to heel the boat out into deeper water by reducing the effective draught, but this is no good with a bilgekeeler, as Fig 31 shows.

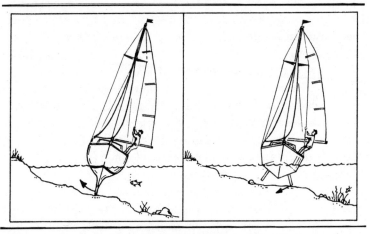

Fig 31 Static heeling. (*Left*) jib aback to blow bow round as crew's weight heels boat; (*Right*) bilgekeelers increase their draught when heeled, and reduce it when upright

61

If you cannot get off instantly, almost as a reflex action, the added power of a reversed propeller *may* do the trick, assisted perhaps by a little punting or even a man over the side to heave on the bows. No one should go casually over the side, but if a man is told off to go, he must wear buoyancy and keep well clear of the propeller. If the boat floats off, he will have to be got aboard, and this may not be as simple as it sounds. The tender can be used to pick him up if needs be.

Once you know that your boat is not going to come off, a running motor should be shut down at once, for it will suck sand and weed into the cooling system. Also, sand violently stirred and waterblasted against the hull can strip paint and damage gel-coat.

Now only manual effort remains to attempt to prevent a *sewing*. A combination of heeling, pushing and pulling may be successful. Swing the boom outboard and hang weights on the end of it—anchors, chain, crewmen, pails of water—anything to achieve some heel. Once she lists, the weight of an agile man up the mast will exert a great heeling moment. Any sort of implement that will reach the ground can be used for shoving. If a kedge can be taken out in the tender, or perhaps walked out, a purchase can be applied to its warp with good effect.

A handy-billy (Fig 32) is invaluable for this and many other purposes and one should be carried aboard every boat. These tackles can be bought ready made up but are easily rove by anyone who can splice a line. Commercial models are usually fitted with a snapshackle at each end, but rope tails of about 18in are much more versatile. They can be hitched to anything, and it is especially useful to be able to put a rolling hitch on a warp, which is not feasible with snapshackles.

Assume that all efforts have failed and you are now fast with some time to wait for the returning tide. There is plenty to do. The bilgekeeler is not in too awkward a position, so let us first consider the dilemma of the finkeeler.

A fall of water exceeding the boat's draught means that she is going to be high and dry before long. If there is anything of a slope to the ground, she must be heeled shoreward. Up to now efforts have been made to heel her outwards and she has to be humped over before the drop in waterlevel makes this impossible.

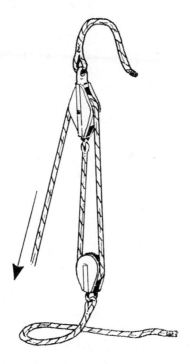

Fig 32 3:1 handy-billy with rope tails instead of hooks.

This is where the whole crew may have to go over the side to heave her over; buoyancy is not needed as the water is becoming shallower. Again, a weighted boom or a kedge can be used if you can rig them in time. If she cannot be rocked over, the hull may lie so steeply down that it will not lift enough before rising water gets over coamings and perhaps down into the bilges. At best this will be uncomfortable and in the extreme can be hazardous. However, all is not yet lost.

A leg or some form of shoring can be placed on the seaward side of the hull to prop her up, and no time should be lost in attempting this. If it is too late, and she will clearly lie on her side, she must be given as much protection as possible.

Anything which will act as a buffer between ground and hull should be put in the obvious places of contact—fenders, bunk cushions, sailbags and so on. Some delving in the water is needed to see that there are no rocks or snags which could pierce the hull. If there are, they might be movable, but if not, they should be guarded against with plenty of padding, such as floorboards, bunkboards, and jetsam timber, which will spread what would otherwise be a point load. The bigger the area over which the weight of the hull can be spread, the less likely a puncture.

All movable objects above and below decks should be lashed or stowed. It is astonishing how far over a boat will lie when dried right out, and how much movable gear and equipment is to be found aboard the average cruiser.

Having made all possible preparation to ensure the safety of your vessel, you then need to calculate how much water is to be expected on the next tide, and when it will arrive. See p 143 for the method of doing this. Stranding some time after the top of a tide usually leads to no difficulty in successfully refloating later. Once this happens you will not want to drift onshore again, and a kedge should be laid out to seaward. It should be carefully positioned, as streams can run hard and erratically, especially in shoal waters. It might be expedient to minimise movement with two anchors taken out at an angle to one another from fore and aft. All that remains is to wait—the time can profitably be employed in inspecting the hull or even scrubbing off, if you have any puff left after the panic!

If there is any doubt about the ability of the next tide to float her, work is needed. A channel can be cleared seaward for the keel to ride along. If she went really hard on and the keel is partly buried, the channel must be dug so that the keel slips into it as she rises, but take care that such grubbing does not cause her to shift bodily, with danger to hull or digger. A heavy anchor must be taken out and dug well in so that a strong and steady pull can be taken on it at the critical moment.

If she lies on hard ground which cannot be grubbed away, you will have to arrange (Fig 33) to haul down on the mast to reduce effective draught when the time is right.

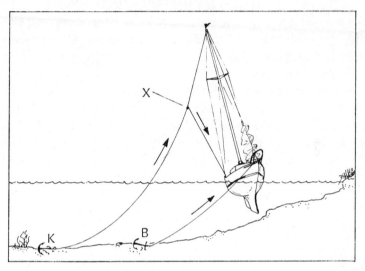

Fig 33 Hauling off a lee shore. The kedge (K) is used to heel her and the bower (B) to haul her off. X=block

Last of all you can think about lightening ship. Really heavy gear can be ferried ashore or put into the tender. Watertanks should be pumped empty. Crew members weigh about twelve to the ton and should be temporarily marooned if this is going to make all the difference to refloating. This is naturally unacceptable in bad weather, and they should, in any case, be fully protected.

If, despite everything you can possibly do, there is a fear of a failure to refloat, you will have to try to arrange for some sort of tug to stand by just before high water—something powerful enough to deliver a few hefty jerks in the right direction at the right time. Time is money to tugmen, so do not let yours start to strain on the towline until the water is full high. The tow will cost you a few pounds, which may be recoverable from your insurance anyway, but better that than a beneaping with sleepless nights and incalculable consequences.

TAKING THE GROUND

You may wish to dry your boat out for a number of reasons, and it is convenient to stand her either against a wall or pile or on open ground. In any case you must position and balance her so that she comes to no harm.

Any object which is statically balanced will have its centre of gravity (CG) vertically above the point, or area, on which it rests (Fig 34). If the body is shifted so that a line dropped perpendicularly from the CG falls outside that area, it will topple. The same thing will happen if the CG is moved inside the object.

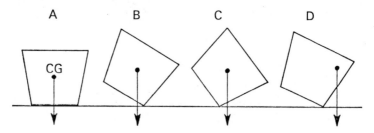

Fig 34 Centre of gravity. Stable (A); will return to stable (B); and unstable (C and D)

Some extreme boats have a vestigial fin keel and their CG lies forward of the lowest point. In this case the craft will not stand on the base of the keel and there is a tendency for it to tilt forward, as shown in Fig 35(i) (exaggerated for clarity). Luckily most boats are more conservative in design and will be stable fore and aft when resting on their keels.

We are more concerned with athwartships stability, where the area of contact is limited by the width of the base of the keel.

A boat cannot be left to stand unaided, as the position of the CG is affected by crew movements, stowage arrangements and outside factors like the pressure of wind on the hull and rigging. It is usual to fit a pair of legs when you want to stand your boat on open ground. Their effect is to broaden the effective area of contact so that the CG can never fall outside it. See Fig 35(ii).

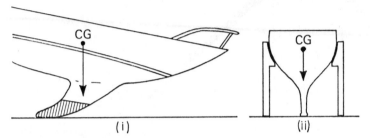

Fig 35 Use of legs. CG=centre of gravity

As long as a boat is not more than a couple of degrees off the vertical, a surprisingly small weight is placed on the legs. Nonetheless, legs should be stoutly made and securely attached to ensure against their breaking in such unforeseen circumstances as going through a crust of mud into a soft patch. If possible, the ground should, of course, be inspected beforehand.

Legs are usually bolted through apertures in the topsides which are locally strengthened; when idle, they are plugged with plates or screwed blanks. The upper parts of the legs are shaped to the round of the hull and padded to prevent damage to paint or gelcoat. They should not be designed to bear on the underside of the caprail, as it might pull away.

Once shipped, legs should be guyed (Fig 36) so that fore and aft movement is prevented. The guylines may be permanently rove to the lower ends of the legs, but it makes for tidier stowage if they are cleated on each time of use. They should be taken well fore and aft with just enough tension to immobilise the legs. Too much tension will tend to pull them in under the bilge and strain the holding bolts and mountings.

67

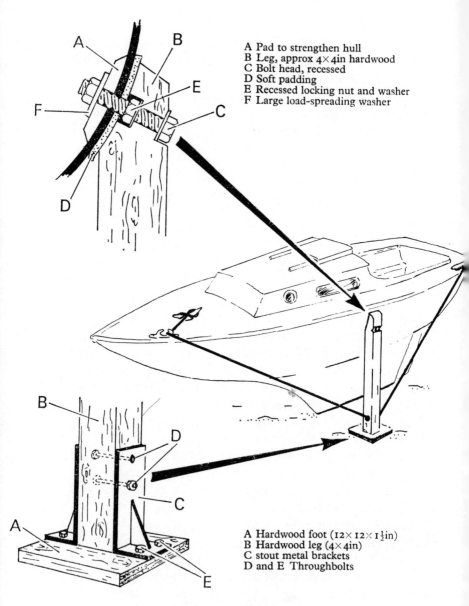

A Pad to strengthen hull
B Leg, approx 4×4in hardwood
C Bolt head, recessed
D Soft padding
E Recessed locking nut and washer
F Large load-spreading washer

A Hardwood foot (12× 12× 1½in)
B Hardwood leg (4×4in)
C stout metal brackets
D and E Throughbolts

Fig 36   Design of legs

Once in place the legs should come to within some 2–3in above the level of the bottom of the keel, which will usually sink that far into anything except rock. It helps to fit feet, as illustrated, to spread the load and these can also be made adjustable for height. Feet are very useful on soft ground to prevent the legs sinking in.

Leadline and sounding pole should be used to see that unfamiliar ground chosen is reasonably level, equally firm on both sides and free from rocks or holes. The boat can be carefully and accurately positioned by the use of two or more anchors if she is likely to range about before touching. If you intend to leave her to look after herself for more than a tide, she should be moored foursquare to rise and fall vertically over the chosen plot. Sufficient scope must be allowed for the highest water anticipated.

It is often possible to lay your boat against a wall, when legs are not normally needed. She should list gently inward with plenty of fenders interposed between hull and wall. Boats which tilt forward on drying are not handy to dry out unless supported with a leg on the seaward side. Its mounting should be far enough forward of the CG for her balance not to be affected if someone walks forward into the bows.

It is unwise to assume that all ground in harbours is suitable for drying out; rocks, foul ground, snags, wrecks and the like are to be found. Gaps in trots often indicate underwater hazards and an enquiry of the harbourmaster should be made beforehand if you are doubtful. Chart readings of an unfamiliar harbour should be treated with reserve, as much activity takes place and is not seen in *Notices to Mariners* until a later date. The safeguards, once again, are leadline, sounding pole and commonsense.

Tying up alongside calls for the use of fore and aft warps (head and stern lines), springs to back them up if there is a stream, fenders and a plank to reinforce them if the wall is rough or lined with projecting piles or buttresses. You will be well advised to arrive in plenty of time with enough water under your keel to permit unhurried preparation. Fore and aft warps should be as long as is dictated by the range of tide (Fig 37), or they will call for frequent tending.

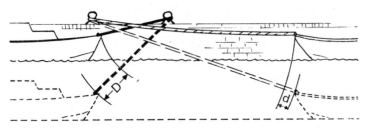

Fig 37 Length of warps. (*Left*) short scope—warp needs to be lengthened by distance D; (*Right*) long scope—distance d shorter than D for same fall of water

Springs are laid out shorter than head and stern lines but, again, they should be long enough to obviate constant adjustment. A spring is belayed aft and taken forward to the wall, and vice versa. These lines control surging by positioning the boat so that the stream does not cause one main warp to be taut and the other fully slack, when the boat would tend to swing out into the stream. Breastropes are lines taken thwartwise ashore from fore and aft. As their purpose is to hold a boat close in, they are not absolutely necessary when drying out, and will be an embarrassment if the deck drops below quay level at any time.

It is not sensible to leave your boat to dry out unattended, as the critical time to achieve good stability is when the keel just starts to feel the ground. It is then essential to see that the boat leans gently inwards; this can be brought about by crew movement and gentle pully-hauly on the wall. An excessive angle of list must be avoided, as if the ground slopes down away from the wall and is at all slippery, the boat may slide as her weight begins to bear on it.

Any offshore wind which might arise must not be allowed to blow the boat away from the wall when she is dry, which could happen if it blows hard and she is very delicately balanced. A line around the mast and belayed ashore will stop this occurring, but it has to take account of rise and fall. A simple method is to reeve a stout halyard through a becketed block and then cleat it tautly up and down the mast. A line tailed on to the block is belayed ashore and will travel up and down the halyard without tending as long as it leads clear of shrouds and other obstructions.

Drying out against a single pile calls for care and knowledge of your boat's characteristics, particularly the position of the CG along the fore and aft line. If this lies any distance from the point of contact between hull and pile, a turning moment will be set up, tending to slew the boat around the pile. A keel which sinks into soft ground will help counter this tendency, but hard ground is suspect if at all slippery. Kedges can be taken out fore and aft at rightangles to the hull and dug in behind the pile, and the tension on their warps should be adjusted to hold the boat evenly against it.

GROUND TACKLE

All owners should carry suitable and reliable ground tackle and know how to use it properly. This is in the interests of safety, for, as a last resort, you may have to anchor off a nasty lee shore. Also, intelligent use of ground tackle permits one to visit many places otherwise denied or ignored because of poor shore facilities. Aside from harbours which dry out, many are overcrowded, noisy, dirty and expensive. A comfortable anchorage in a quiet cove nearby can provide more relaxation and enjoyment and still be within reach of the bright lights.

The best anchors for use on small boats are the CQR and Meon (formerly called Danforth). For a given weight their holding power is much greater than the traditional 'fisherman', although this holds better on rocky ground and where weed lies thick on the seabed. One could be carried if a passage is going to take in such ground. Anchoring on either type of ground is to be avoided if possible, as an anchor may drag or jam in a crevice when laid on rock and fail to hold at all among thick weed.

It is not possible to be dogmatic about the sizes of anchors, as the drag of a boat will depend on her characteristics, but, as an indication, it might be suitable to equip a 5-tonner with a 25lb bower and a 12lb kedge. In choosing a bower it is best to err on the heavy side. The kedge should be about half the weight of the bower and, in addition to purposes already mentioned, can be used for temporary anchoring in fine weather. All ground tackle is expensive, so it is as well to avoid making mistakes in initial purchase.

As there is little difference, weight for weight, in the holding power of the CQR and the Meon, the deciding factor in your choice will probably be ease of handling and of stowage. The genuine articles have been proved reliable, but there are many imitations on the market which should be viewed with caution. They can be of inferior metal and not conform to the carefully designed dimensions of the original patterns. Although probably a bit cheaper, they may lack integrity and holding power, and one day your safety may rest on these qualities in your tackle.

In smaller boats it is often difficult to handle anchors through the pulpit. Meon anchors present problems here, although otherwise they lie flatter and are a bit easier to handle and stow than the CQR, with its awkwardly shaped and freely pivoted blade.

Anchor stowage

The stowage of anchors should be given full consideration. While it is handy to have an anchor stowed on the foredeck ready for immediate use, this could well be the kedge; the bower could be stowed away in the bilge, providing it can be roused out easily and fairly quickly. In small craft it is advisable to keep heavy weights as low down as possible in the hull in the interests of stability. Special chocks are available if deck stowage is decided on; if these are fitted, they should be throughbolted. If they are just screwed down, a sheet may one day snag under the anchor and tear everything loose.

Chain and rope

Over the ages anchors have been secured with rope, wrought iron, and galvanised and steel chains. Today's synthetic warps provide an efficient alternative to chain, which natural rope could not do. Whatever sort of warp you use must be of the right size and of reputable manufacture.

Chain tolerates chafe at stemhead and on seabed, and, as it hangs in a deep catenary, exerts a horizontal pull on the anchor if adequate scope is used. The inertia of chain helps to damp out surging. It is easy to run out and to stow. Against this it is heavy to handle and to stow, and heavy weights right up forward where most chainlockers are situated are best avoided. Only chain certified as tested should be bought; the stud link variety is stronger than open link, but considerably more expensive.

Length for length and strength for strength synthetic rope is cheaper than chain, and reputable stuff is reliable all through. It is much lighter than chain but more difficult to handle and stow. It should really be coiled on a reel for ease of handling, but the stowage and mounting of these on small boats is an intractable problem.

Rope warps lie in a shallow catenary which pulls out easily when the boat surges. In order to maintain a horizontal pull on the anchor it is necessary to have 3–4 fathoms of chain next to it. This also takes the scrape of the seabed, but means have to be devised to prevent the warp chafing over the stemhead. Here is a good tip.

Every 4 fathoms along your warp, which will later be seen to correspond to a depth of water of 1 fathom, make a spliced eye with a short piece of the same rope. Fit a round thimble snugly into each eye—by making the eye quite a bit smaller than the thimble, hammering it down over a tapered fid and inserting the thimble as soon as the fid is knocked out of the eye. This has to be done smartly before the rope contracts, but is a knack soon picked up by a handy man.

73

Having decided on the scope to be used at any time, shackle a couple of fathoms of chain into the appropriate thimble. The chain lies over the stemhead and is belayed to the samsonpost. Not only will it prevent any chafe on the warp but will lower it sufficiently in the water to keep it away from passing propellers and snags. If the end of the chain is fitted with a strop (Fig 8) and only just brought over the stemhead, damage to the deck surface will be eliminated.

Although terylene is marginally stronger, nylon is preferable for anchor warps on account of its elasticity. Floating ropes such as polypropylene will assume a reverse catenary which exerts a lifting effort on the anchor. Such rope is also stiffer than nylon, harder on the hands and not as strong.

Security

Weaknesses in ground tackle lie in points of connection and attachment, where the use of shackles is universal. Snapshackles and other types which do not make a fully closed loop are not safe to use at any time, and unless you join lengths of a chain with proper chain-joining shackles, use the screwpin model. All shackle pins *must* be moused by passing a short length of wire a couple of times through the eye of the pin, then round the leg of the shackle and twisting it together. The metals of chain, thimbles, shackles and mousing wire should all be compatible to prevent electrolytic action. Copper wire and bronze shackles (and please make very sure that no one ever sells you brass ones) will strip off galvanising and attack the iron beneath very quickly in a salty environment. If it is your custom to keep an anchor ready shackled on forward—an excellent habit—the mousing should be watched for wear and damage.

Shackles used on ground tackle should be of the 'D' type and not the 'bow'. The legs of the shackles should fit as snugly as possible over the links of the chain and the pin should be as large as will enter them.

The end of any anchor cable must be secured inboard to prevent accidental runout and loss over the side, complete with anchor. The end of scope of a warp should be belayed before the anchor is put over to prevent a pull on the reel and its mounting. The warp should also be made fast to the reel at its inner end.

Chain should be secured to a strongpoint in the locker—a ringbolt through a bulkhead or frame, perhaps. It is a good idea to end the chain in a stout lanyard which will render through the chainpipe and on to the deck. If it is ever necessary for you to jettison your ground tackle because it is fouled solid, or because you have to cut and run, it is far easier to sever a line than dash below and release a shackle in the bowels of the chainlocker. You may have to stand on your head and it will inevitably be rusted solid.

Scope
Scope is the length of cable required to anchor safely; it depends on depth of water and prevailing conditions. It is explained later (p 80) how scope is calculated. For now suffice it to say that you should not carry less than 30 fathoms of cable *for each anchor*. Experience will show whether you need more for any reason, but joined lengths are not as strong as integral ones, so give this matter your fullest attention before spending your cash. Ideally you should carry one length of chain and one of warp.

Maintenance
Synthetic rope is immensely durable if properly cared for. It tolerates constant immersion, a wide range of temperature and is impervious to marine corrosion. Some ropes are attacked by acids or alkalis and suppliers will advise on this. All types will chafe on sharp edges, glaze if heated over a certain temperature, either by friction or other causes, and will, like any other rope, deteriorate if sand and grit are allowed to remain inside the lay. A swill out with fresh water and a shampoo with mild detergent will bring them up like new. Nylon is very elastic, and can be taken to 120 per cent of its length before it parts, which makes it very

useful for an anchor warp; but it lets go and recoils violently. Terylene can only be extended about 3 per cent of its length before breaking.

Chain may lose its galvanising, and then a coat of something like Kurust or Galvafroid may be applied for a certain degree of protection. In bad cases regalvanising can be done by a specialist firm; it is usually charged for by weight. Grease is removed in the price, but removal of paint from a chain costs extra. Links can be distorted through careless belaying or undue strain, and they become thin with use. If there is doubt about the quality of any chain, suspect lengths can be sawn out and the sound lengths remaining married up with proper chain-joining shackles.

Damage to the galvanising of anchors can be dealt with similarly. They should be inspected periodically for distortion or fracture, and wear in the eye to which the cable shackles. Amateur repairs to anchors are ill advised, and a specialist firm will say whether it is more economical to renew rather than try to remedy defects. Do not hesitate to discard a suspect anchor.

Handling

An anchor not laid with care and attention can run away to the full length of chain, which will then pile up on top of it. Any attempt to stop a runaway anchor is simply inviting injury and loss of fingers. Let it go and recover the excess scope later.

A warp running away is not so lethal as chain, but can snare unwary legs; it can also get into a terrible snarl. It is wise to surge a cable around a post or large cleat, when friction will allow good control.

Sail around twice and anchor once. Fumbled anchoring causes doubled effort and the work is heavy. In choosing an anchorage remember that the boat will fall back to the end of her scope and may swing into an undesired position if you have not considered wind and stream.

When using chain it is convenient to range out the required scope in parallel lengths on the deck and belay the end. It helps greatly to mark the chain with a simple code to indicate each 5 fathoms, something like this:

5fm	1 red painted link
10fm	1 white painted link
15fm	1 blue painted link
20fm	2 red painted links
25fm	2 white painted links

and so on. The sequence of red, white and blue is easy to remember.

Having arrived at the spot where the anchor is to lie, bring your craft stationary in relation to the ground. As she starts to make a little sternway, lower the anchor carefully to the ground and let out about half the scope; then belay. Once the anchor is felt to bite, let out the remaining scope right to its belay. Gathering sternway should dig it home, but you may have to use a reversed motor in calm weather with no streams. If you cannot do this, beware of piling the chain on top of the anchor, as it may foul and cause trouble later.

Having laid the anchor, you must see that it is not dragging, which is simply done by observing a transit or taking bearings of a handy object ashore. If bad visibility does not permit this, lower the lead over the side to rest lightly on the ground. Any movement of the boat will drag the weight along the seabed, and this is felt distinctly in the line.

In less leisurely times it may be urgent to get an anchor down with the boat still under way. Try first to slow her with bucket or other drogue. If possible, get a reasonable scope belayed, but in extremity you may have to let the whole chain run out and recover it later to the proper scope. As chain runs out so much more easily than rope, it is preferable to warp in emergency and, of course, an anchor already shackled in saves valuable time.

Weighing anchor
The rigours of weighing anchor may be the determining factor

in the final choice of a boat to suit its minimum crew. Before a heavy anchor and chain can be weighed, there is the backbreak of hauling the boat up to short stay and then perhaps having to break out an anchor which has dug in almost immovably. Winches are a godsend, but if you do not have one, help can be had from purchases and a stemhead pawl (Fig 38).

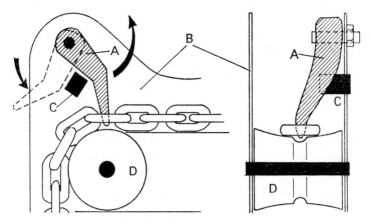

Fig 38   Use of chain pawl

A Chain pawl   C Pawl stop
B Side plate   D Roller

Anchor winches are costly, weighty and mostly so cumbersome as to be unacceptable on a small foredeck. Sheet and halyard winches should never be used for anchor work, as they will not take the strain and will sooner or later be damaged or pull adrift.

In bad conditions manual effort usually means snatching in a short length of cable as the bows dip, belaying it before they lift again, and repeating the operation as long as necessary. It can take an age to raise a fathom. It is then that the value of a simple stemhead pawl is realised, as this automatically belays each hard-won inch of chain. Rope cannot be so handled.

Chain should run down clear through the chainpipe, and you should take pains to see that, in fact, it does so. Many pipes are too narrow to be practical, and some are so ill sited and fitted that the chain jams in both directions. Sometimes a plastic pipe or wooden guide leads from the underside of the deck down to the locker, its purpose being to lead the chain through a sail locker and on down into the chain compartment below it. If the pipe is too small, it will certainly prevent an easy run of chain, and should either be removed or replaced with one of adequate diameter.

If not on a reel, rope has to be coiled each time after use. When conditions do not allow this to be done, the warp ends up in a great bunch of bights which have to be sorted out later.

Once weighed and sighted, the anchor can be left lying over the stemhead as a temporary measure, but its cable must be firmly taken back and belayed. It may also be necessary to lash the anchor to the stemhead with a short piece of line to prevent jumping. Unless firmly secured it may run out again with incalculable results.

Ideally, an anchor and cable should be washed down during weighing. If this cannot be done, and they have been down in mud or ooze, they should all be left on deck if possible for the time being. If taken into the chainlocker such muck will dry off, smell terrible and be difficult to remove.

Laying an anchor

An anchor must be laid so that it holds reliably until deliberately weighed. The first thing to think about is the ability of the ground to accept and grip the anchor, ie how good is the holding ground? I have mentioned that rocky and weedy bottoms are not satisfactory, but if you have to let go in such ground, frequent checks must be made for dragging. Clay and hard sand let an anchor dig well in and hold firmly. Looser sand, shingle and mud in its various forms are less secure and, although you may seem well held, a rising wind or increasing stream can start you dragging. In suspect ground the heavier the anchor used the better.

A boat on a tidal anchorage will swing on her cable with ebb and flow so that the pull on the anchor is periodically reversed. The worse the ground the more likely an anchor will be to emerge and redig itself in after slack water. Before it gets home again the boat may drift some distance, and a watch should be kept at the turn of each tide.

If you use a 'fisherman' in shallow water, make sure that you do not impale your boat on the upper fluke as the water falls. It sounds silly, but it does happen from time to time at slack water. Also, care should be taken not to pile chain on top of a 'fisherman', as it is very liable to foul.

As mentioned, an anchor will only hold reliably if the pull of the cable is horizontal; any vertical component of pull will tend to lift it out of the ground. A satisfactory pull cannot be exerted unless there is sufficient scope. This should never be less than three times the depth of water for chain and four for rope. In unfavourable weather when a boat will be driven hard enough to flatten the catenary of the cable, or with poor holding ground, it is essential to use more than minimum scope. It follows from this that the remedy for a dragging anchor is to let out more cable and not to shorten in. This may seem a disconcerting action if your craft is dragging into an obstruction such as a boat astern, but incorrect action will only make matters worse.

Depth of water
To calculate the depth of water to be met with during a period of anchoring you must know the state of the tide on arrival. Tidal tables are given in almanacs and elsewhere, and the full calculations are given in Chapter 3. When anchoring off a beach, say, one has to stand off a bit to allow for an inshore swing, and it would be usual to anchor in about 2 fathoms or so. If this is at low water and the tidal rise is a not uncommon 18ft, the *minimum* scope should be 15 fathoms of chain or 20 fathoms of warp. More is needed for insurance and this is why a minimum of 30 fathoms was previously recommended. One popular cruiser is advertised as 'complete with 22fm of nylon warp'. It is difficult to see how this figure was arrived at.

Anticipation

Anchorages normally only give shelter against winds from a limited arc, and an eye must be kept on the possibility of changing conditions. If you are sheltering from a blow, the passage of the weather system responsible will carry with it a perceptible, and perhaps sudden, shift of wind. Unless your chosen haven protects you from both the existing and expected winds, you should make ready to shift your ground. Some headlands and small islands provide refuges on different sides, eg Dungeness or St Mary's.

Changes in tidal streams or currents should be considered in like manner when you are thinking of anchoring for any reason.

Mooring

Changes in natural conditions cause a boat to swing on the end of her scope, and the swinging circle can be quite large. It can be cut down considerably if you use two anchors to moor with (Fig 39).

The second anchor can be taken out in a tender or laid by using the manoeuvre known as a running moor. One anchor is laid and its cable paid out smartly while the boat sails on to the point where the second one is to be dropped. The craft is then dropped back astern and the cables adjusted so that she lies equally between the anchors. Alternatively you can secure your boat by laying one anchor with excess scope and sailing her around the perimeter of the swinging circle to the point of laying the second. Either method needs plenty of practice, preferably in fine weather, when resulting tangles of cable and routines can be sorted out and corrected for future use. In addition to reducing the swinging circle a running moor holds a boat far more securely.

Backing up an anchor

If the size of circle is immaterial, the holding power of an anchor can be augmented in several ways. A traveller (heavy weight) can be slid down the cable on a light line to within a couple of

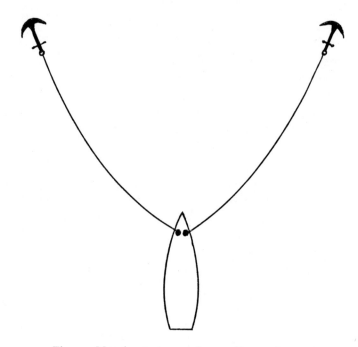

Fig 39   Mooring to two anchors, with equal scopes

fathoms of the anchor. This damps surging by increasing inertia, and also holds the cable nearer the horizontal. Specially designed travellers are marketed but other things can be used; occasions for use are likely to be infrequent and large expenditure is hardly justified. A large ship's shackle can be kept in the bilge in case of need. This has a very convenient shape to slip around a cable. The kedge can be sent down with a bight taken around the cable with a short line. Another way of increasing the power of a single anchor is to lay it in tandem with the kedge (Fig 40).

Fouled anchor
An anchor may foul under a cable, old mooring chain, wreck or other obstacle, or just jam in a crevice. Any anchor laid should be buoyed beforehand. A light line is made fast to the crown of

the anchor—usually a ring is fitted there for the purpose—and paid out with the cable. It should be long enough to permit the small buoy shackled at its other end to float at high water. This buoy should be as small as will support the weight of its line and be distinctively marked 'Anchor buoy'. If it is not, and if it has a handle, it will sooner or later be lifted by another boat in search of a mooring, which is tedious for all concerned.

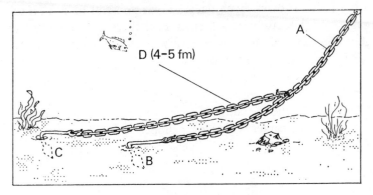

Fig 40 Backing up an anchor

A Main cable   C Kedge
B Bower anchor   D Chain shackled to main cable

A steady strain on the buoy line will often free a fouled anchor. If this does not work, you must try to find out what is fouling the anchor. If it has pulled under a cable or like object on the seabed, it may be possible to lift the obstruction a little. The anchor cable should be hove in taut and belayed. A weighted line can then perhaps be dropped over the obstruction, fished out from the opposite side and brought inboard. If it is then tautly belayed, the anchor may drop free when its cable is slacked off. It may be necessary to wait for the water to drop before you can get at the obstruction. If it is too heavy to lift manually, the anchor cable may lift it if it is made very taut at low water and kept that way as the water rises.

A stubbornly fouled anchor can often be freed if the boat is sailed over and past it so that the pull comes from the opposite direction. Some scope can usefully be taken in before the boat snubs at the end of travel.

If the anchor is not fouled but just dug in very hard, the boat's own buoyancy can be used to free it if there is a scend to the water. The cable is taken in taut and belayed. Each time the bows dip it should be possible to snatch in some cable and hold with a belay or pawl. Eventually a great pull will be put on the anchor and, hopefully, it will emerge. If there is no scend, once again you can wait for low water, belay taut on the cable and wait for the rising tide to free you.

Slipping

If all else fails, the anchor may have to be slipped, together with all or part of its cable. Whatever is slipped should be buoyed and its position carefully fixed. A diver can recover it later.

CHAPTER TWO

Basic Navigation

INTRODUCTORY

At any moment during a passage a navigator is liable to be asked
to give the boat's position. He should always find himself able to
give a ready and reliable answer. He may also be asked for a
course to steer, an estimated time of arrival at a certain position
(ETA), depth of water to be anticipated at an anchorage, and
many other such things. In the final analysis it will be found that
nearly all the answers are based on his knowledge of the present
position.

The basic navigation needed for our modest passage-making
is really quite an uncomplicated affair, but it calls for a little
knowledge, accurate observation, meticulous attention to detail
and the ability to use a few simple instruments. Without these
you may lead your boat into danger, and navigation is best defined
as the ability to guide a boat from place to place *in safety*.

We are only going to concern ourselves in these pages with
getting along a coastline and making relatively short passages
offshore. Celestial navigation is neither needed nor discussed.
Part of the business that can present problems to the uninitiated
navigator, who is probably the skipper of any small boat as well,
is taking her up to and into harbours. This is usually known as
pilotage, and is dealt with in detail in the next chapter. As a
matter of passing interest, the word has biblical origins and stems
from 'peil-loth', which means lead and line—for many centuries
the only means of ascertaining the depth of water available to the
mariner.

Chart reading
A chart is a pictorial representation of an area of water and any
bordering land. Ability to relate a chart to its corresponding
area, and the reverse process, is the first requirement of a navigator. The standard reference work for most of the world is the
British Admiralty chart No 5011, a listing of all the navigational
markings used on charts produced by the Hydrographer to the
Royal Navy. Other publishers of charts habitually use the same
symbols and I take the liberty of quoting from *Reed's Almanac*,
whose views on the subject could not be better or more wisely
expressed:

> Owing to the considerable number of such symbols now
> employed on Admiralty charts (and for safety's sake used on other
> charts) it is not possible or sensible to try to commit them all to
> memory. It is infinitely preferable to try to remember the really
> important signs and to be able to turn instantly to the list to see
> what any symbol means.

This wisdom applies not only to charts but to nearly all navigational information. A navigator is not a memory man, and only
needs to know where to turn for the information needed for use
at any time.

Marks
Charts show that busy coasts are plentifully studded with land-
marks and sea marks, each of which conveys a message to the
mariner. By night their structures become invisible, but important ones exhibit a light of individual character. Lights shine and
blink in many fashions and you will have to get used to observing
a light and saying to yourself 'Yes, that is the one marked on
the chart as "Gp Fl (3) ev 5 secs".'
It is relatively easy, by day, to judge whether a mark is distant
or close to and to take its bearing. In the dark things are not
quite so simple, and two points need to be stressed straightaway.

Any light, to be of use, must be *unmistakably* identified; in some sea conditions this can be difficult to do. Importantly, *distance off a light can never be estimated by eye*. A distant powerful beam may shine much more brightly than a dim but nearer one, and only its bearing can be determined with accuracy.

Buoyage systems
Buoys are the principal aid to the coastal navigator, and the standard system for your own country is one of the things that certainly should be committed to memory. The message conveyed instantly by the shape, colour, topmark, light and other characteristics of a buoy makes for steady confident progress without the need to refer to chart or book. Full details are given in relevant literature such as almanacs, but a couple of points are worth a mention here.

Total reliance should never be reposed in buoys. They can break adrift, sink, lose their lights, and be subject to continual change about, alteration and removal, and their swinging circle can be quite large if they are laid in deep water. Not for the last time your attention is drawn to the fact that only *up-to-date* charts and other navigational information are safe to be used.

Except for those marking isolated dangers such as wrecks and pinnacles arising from the seabed, buoys are usually moored in areas of comparatively shallow water. However, buoyage systems are designed primarily for large vessels and there will often be enough water for small craft to stray outside the marked channels in safety. This should not be done without close attention to the chart on every occasion, for many buoys lie close to ledges, steep shelves, rocks and shoals. It is folly to close a buoy about whose function and location you are in doubt.

Main systems, including the British system, are based on an arbitrary Main Flood Stream. The thing to be remembered by coastal sailors is that such a stream flows *into* all openings such as rivers, estuaries and harbours. **Buoys designated as Starboard Hand or Port Hand are to be left on that side of the**

boat when entering from seaward. On departure starboard hand buoys are left to port and vice versa.

In creeks, small harbours and places not navigable by ships the buoyage systems will, in general, copy the principal scheme, but the marks themselves may not be so prominent or well marked and will in many cases be unlighted. Many helpful guides and locally written handbooks deal with these out-of-the-way places and are useful to carry aboard. Such things as withies, perches, beacons and small spars are obviously stuck into the ground, and it is advisable to keep well clear of them and not stray outside the bounds of the channel they define. If they are set on soft ground, you may find that with the passage of time some of them are well inshore of navigable water.

European countries in particular use what is known as the Cardinal System of marking dangers. It has much to recommend it, but it would be better to refresh your memory before each visit than to try to remember its details. Channel markings can be expected to remain constant within the boundaries of any one country, but can vary in detail as one sails on to an adjoining one.

Sound signals
When visibility is seriously impeded, the place of markers and lights is often taken by foghorns, whistles, bells and other sounds. These can be static ashore and static or moving at sea. The positions and characteristics of sound signals are given in relevant lists and in almanacs, and sounds made by vessels are prescribed in the Collision Rules. The use of fog signals is tricky, as both intensity and apparent bearing can be misleading. Only practical experience at sea will serve to show up their value and their limitations.

Traffic rules
The International Regulations for Preventing Collisions at Sea apply to all vessels afloat, regardless of size or purpose. Too long to reproduce here, they are to be found in navigational books and almanacs. There are not only ethical and practical reasons why

yachtsmen should abide by them, but compelling legal ones. They have been developed as the result of countless years of experience, and exist solely in the interests of the safety of all souls at sea. Ignorance or disregard of the Collision Rules, as they are usually termed, many cause damage, injury or loss of life. The Master who is to blame will have to bear a heavy responsibility, which may impose not only a burden of guilt and remorse but severe financial penalties. This may sound dire and dreary, but sailing is a serious business fundamentally, no matter how enjoyable.

Crewmen, essentially helmsmen and navigators, should try to memorise the rules. As an *aide-memoire* a pictorial record of lights to be met with at sea can be permanently mounted above the chart table.

Despite right-of-way conferred under the Rules, a vulnerable yacht should take avoiding action if there is the slightest chance of a collision with a ship. This should be done in such a way that your intention is made unmistakably clear in plenty of time, so that a belated realisation of the situation and a correction to course by the larger vessel will not make matters worse. It would be unrealistic to ignore the fact that many steamers in traffic lanes either do not notice, or choose to disregard, the existence and rights of yachts in their vicinity.

Conventions

A navigator will have to mark his charts on passage, and it is sensible to use the conventional terms and signs in common use. No problems or doubts will then arise on change of watch as to what navigation has been carried out up to that time. Loose usage of certain terms can give rise to confusion at times, so that it is as well to treat the matter now. The following definitions are used consistently through this book and fully explained, where necessary, in the first relevant text:

Position: the latitude and longitude of a point or object,

expressed in degrees and minutes, latitude stated first thus—
52° 15′ N: 26° 05′ W.

Knot: 1 nautical mile per hour. A measure of speed. In navigational calculations a period of 1hr is often used as a base, and in such a case the terms knot and nautical mile can be interchanged without confusion.

Mile: at sea this is a nautical mile (nm) of 6,080ft.

Cable: one-tenth of a nautical mile. Often taken as 200yd.

Track: the path described along the seabed of a boat passing through the water above. A proposed track drawn on a chart is sometimes called a **courseline,** but it is confusing to abbreviate this to **course.**

Heading: the direction, from aft to fore, in which a boat is pointing. When expressed in terms which can be put on or taken off a compass card, it may also be known as the **compass course, course to steer** or simply the **course.**

True: degrees expressed with reference to True North. Chart grids normally lie True N, S, E and W. Degrees not suffixed are assumed to be True.

Magnetic: degrees expressed with reference to Magnetic North. Suffixed '(M)', eg 187° (M).

Variation: the difference, in degrees and direction, between True and Magnetic at a given position.

Compass: a steering instrument. Compass degrees are those read on the compass card. Suffixed '(C)', eg 123° (C).

Deviation: the difference, in degrees and direction, between Magnetic and Compass for a given heading.

Compass error: the algebraical sum of variation and deviation.

Tidal streams: movements of a body of water caused by tidal conditions. These are often wrongly termed **currents,** especially in rivers and estuaries affected by tides.

Currents: movements of water, usually surface water, caused by other than tides, eg by a wind blowing steadily for a period in a constant direction. Such a current can augment or diminish the effect of a stream with which it combines. There are strong,

major standing currents to be found, such as the Gulf Stream
and Mozambique Current.

Rate: the speed of a stream or current.

Set: A stream or current 'sets' in a certain direction as distinct
from a wind which blows *from* a given quarter.

Drift: the distance covered during a specified period by a stream
or current, or by a boat when hove-to or drifting without means
of propulsion.

Vector: a line representing both a force and its direction. In
navigation usually distance and direction.

Signs:

$+$ Dead reckoning position (DR)

$\triangle$ Estimated position (EP)

$\odot$ Fixed position (Fix)

$\rightarrow$ Course of boat

$\twoheadrightarrow$ Track of boat

$\ggg$ Set of stream

Note 1. It is usual to note the time of plotting a position.

Note 2. It is usual to mark both distance and direction along
navigational vectors. Directions must be in the same sort of
degrees, ie do not mix T and M, C and M or T and C.

EQUIPMENT AND ITS USE

Naval charts are normally the standard works for any country
and private publications are based on them. In the UK, Admiralty
charts are sold by agents who have a catalogue from which you
can choose a selection (folio) to suit your purposes. Corrections
to charts are published regularly in *Notices to Mariners*, available
from chart agents and exhibited at Customs Houses for inspection.
You can correct your own charts with the aid of *Notices*, but it is

fiddly work and better done for a small fee by the agent or a specialist firm. Careful timing will enable you to get your charts back as up-to-date as possible just before the season begins.

Admiralty charts are rather large for easy handling aboard a small boat, and it may prove better to use one of the editions specially produced for yachtsmen. It does not matter greatly what sort you use as long as they are kept up-to-date. However, when starting out to buy for the first time, it is sensible to standardise, as familiarity with a format makes for easy use.

One point needs to be thought about. Some charts display both True and Magnetic roses while others limit themselves to a Magnetic one. There are two main ways of working, and the method you adopt will determine your choice of charts.

Any course put on to a steering compass will, obviously, have to be stated in ° (C). This is arrived at by applying deviation to a Magnetic course, which itself can be taken direct from a Magnetic rose or calculated by applying variation to a course taken off a True compass rose.

As explained later, course-setting and position-finding call for the resolution of vectors relating to directions, and these must all be set down in the same sort of degrees. It makes no difference to your results if they are all in ° (T) or ° (M), but a mixture of the two would immediately give rise to error.

Most written information on charts and in almanacs and reference works is given in degrees True, as also are lines printed on charts giving bearings, transits, clearances and so forth. Chart grids are also printed to read True and bear N, S, E and W so that they can be used with the help of a protractor instead of a rose with a rule. Thus, if you extract all information in ° (T) as a habit and then convert it into ° (M) for plotting purposes, your navigation may be easier than the alternative of reading direct from a Magnetic rose and then converting all other information from True to Magnetic. You can see that the latter method could lead you to mix up different sorts of degrees if you were tired or distracted.

Providing your sailing is confined to a fairly restricted area, no matter in what part of the world you may be, conversion from True to Magnetic can be made very simply. For example, in British waters today, and for many years to come, variation is westerly, so the trick is done if you learn one sentence by heart: *True plus variation equals magnetic.*

Life is made even simpler if you restrict yourself to an area in which variation is constant. Your formula could then be distilled to read, for example: *True plus 7° equals magnetic.*

Variation

The simplest possible way of finding out the amount of variation which affects you is to refer to the 'Navigational aids' pages at the back of *Reed's Almanac*. At the bottom of each page is a legend which gives the number of whole degrees of variation for the longitude in question.

Another way is to refer to a double rose on a chart for the area. This will be printed with the variation in degrees and minutes for a given year, together with the annual rate of change. The variation for today can be simply calculated and taken to the nearest whole number of degrees.

Many jingles exist concerning variation and its application which can cause chaos if wrongly remembered. Forget them and work from first principles.

Instruments

Chart work consists of laying off courselines, bearings and position lines, measuring distances, scribing arcs of circles and writing information. The basic instruments are a rule, dividers, pencils, soft eraser and a pair of pencil compasses. A magnifying glass, preferably illuminated, as used by stamp collectors, is almost essential for scrutinising fine type and small figures on the chart.

Parallel rules are difficult to use on a small chart table and have a tendency to slip when being transferred over the chart. Roller rules are easier to use, but avoid heavy brass ones; they can cause damage and injury if adrift in a seaway. I use a simple rule made of a short length of $\frac{1}{2}$in dowelling fitted at each end with one of those rubber endcaps for chairlegs; they are held on with a smear of Araldite. The length can be tailored to fit your own table. I have used mine for years and would have nothing else; they cost next to nothing to make.

As an alternative to some sort of rule, you can use a 45° set square in combination with a straightedge or such things as Douglas protractors and Hurst plotters. Chandlers will let you examine a selection of instruments before making up your mind what to buy, but they may not point out that shiny expensive instruments are not necessarily superior in use to simpler, even homemade, articles.

Soft pencils, about 3B, preserve the surface of charts, and all markings should habitually be removed with a soft eraser as soon as they are finished with. Pencils need good points, so a sharpener or razor blade should lie handy to the chart table. If not jealously guarded, such items will be pinched by sailors for such lower-deck activities as opening tins and trimming toenails.

Good dividers are essential and it is sensible to carry two pairs. It does not matter whether you use the ordinary straightleg model or the 'one-handed' variety, as long as they are rustproof. Choose them of a realistic size, for small ones are frustrating, and for firm and smooth operation. Reject any which are loose, stiff or jerky to operate. Your pencil compasses should be of the schoolboy type into which any old stub of pencil will fit rather than one demanding the insertion of thin and fragile leads. Extreme accuracy is not called for.

Chart table

You cannot work effectively unless you have a chart table big enough to hold a chart folded to a workable size. The table must be firm enough to lean against to write on. Many small boats are only fitted with a collapsible table, but there is no objection to this as long as it is thoughtfully designed. There are those which slide into place, maybe out of a quarterberth, and others which are variously hinged or hung on chains. Whatever type, if fitted, must be proof against accidental collapse. The use of galley working tops is not recommended, as charts will gradually acquire an impenetrable patina of butter and jam.

Chart stowage
Charts should not be rolled, as they acquire a permanent tendency to curl up which makes them difficult to use. They should be folded only to the extent needed to fit them into the confines of the table. They can be laid flat under the driest bunk cushion or slid behind a batten fixed to a bulkhead, but if it is possible to have a special drawer to contain them, life is simpler. About the chart table there should also be some form of racking or shelving to hold books and instruments.

Gen-board
A useful adjunct to chartwork is a gen-board—a piece of stiff ply covered with transparent plastic and open at one side. Into this is slipped information such as notes of local routes, eg from moorings to places frequently visited, deviation charts, beacon frequencies, the High Water Dover card—in fact, any information that is constantly being referred to. The board can hang on a peg or lie flat in a drawer or on a bunk.

A similar board is invaluable to hold any charts which have to be taken on deck, say for conning into harbour. Unless protected from weather and wellingtons their life will be short and dismal. They will also be sopping wet and useless at times when they are urgently needed.

Siting and lighting the table
Attention must be paid to the comfort and other requirements of the navigator. If he has to kneel, crouch or perform incredible contortions to reach the table, his navigation will be unreliable.

Sooner or later you will have to work in poor light or at night, and lighting of the chart table is important. A chart must be so well illuminated that small but vital markings are never missed. Shadows can be avoided if you fit a movable light, and the ones on long flexible stalks are admirable. Independent lighting ensures that any failure of the main circuit does not mean a resort to matches, candles or torches. A dry cell of good capacity will last a whole season on an average boat, and a spare should be kept, together with a spare bulb, in a waterproof container stowed away from possible damage.

If there is a likelihood, as often on a family boat, of the navigator having to dash on deck to cope with a sailing situation, he will need his night sight immediately. This is virtually unaffected by red or orange light and the chart table lamp should be suitably tinted. Coloured nail varnish serves well to cover a plain bulb.

Pilot books
Navigation would hardly be possible without using 'pilots' which are books giving a wide range of facts and figures needed for safe navigation within the area dealt with. Admiralty 'pilots' encompass the whole world in a series of volumes, but these are not tailored to the needs of a small boat owner, and it is often more convenient to use specialised yachtsmen's guides. These are crammed with facts, drawings and photographs of salient features like markers, harbours and their approaches, and assist in correct interpretation of chart data.

Almanacs are compendiums of marine lore, and invaluable for reference. Much of their contents is repeated annually, but ephemeral stuff such as tide and astronomical tables change with each edition. Lists of lights and buoys are up-to-date at the time of publication, but need to be kept corrected, like charts, and this matter is often overlooked.

Tidal stream atlases
Tidal streams affect all coastal navigation and no boat can afford

to be without tidal stream atlases for the areas being sailed over. These give hourly indications of the set and rate of streams for both neap and spring conditions. Interpolation between these states is made with the help of a table given in the atlas. Use care in taking stream data from these booklets; they are small in scale and streams can vary significantly in a short distance, especially close to a coast and around bays and headlands. Charts are marked with letters enclosed in a diamond, eg ⟨B⟩ , or something similar which relate to stream data printed in the form of a table on the chart margin. It is better to use this information when possible, as the larger scale makes it more accurate than a pocket size atlas.

Later on you will see how to use tidal stream data for navigation, but for now just remember that the slower the speed of your boat the more critically its progress will be affected by streams.

Magnetic compasses
Navigation is impossible without a steering compass and difficult without a handbearing model. It pays to choose critically and not to begrudge money spent on compasses. They are precision instruments and must be handled gently, for on their accuracy and reliability rests the safety of your boat and its crew. Any compass which has been dropped or heavily jarred must be regarded as suspect and inspected as soon as possible. A sticky or jerky movement of the card may indicate damage to the jewelled bearings.

Choice of a compass for taste and fitting requirements is a matter for careful consideration. Some like to use card and lubber-line to steer; others a grid or a side-reading card. There is a great variety to be had, and the only real guide to their suitability is to use them under sailing conditions. Lighting is essential and can be either direct or luminous. Paraffin is occasionally used, and is reliable though messy. Electric lighting can be varied in intensity, and tinted red or orange if preferred; it is best independent of the main supply or at least capable of independent illumination in case of failure.

The compass of a sailing boat must be fully gimballed and fairly well damped so that it will not oscillate violently in a seaway. Criteria for compasses are different for sailing and power-craft, so avoid buying the wrong sort. Some ex-service compasses can be used or adapted for use on yachts, but those intended for aircraft are not usually gimballed and may be far too heavily damped. Ex-naval compasses can be expected to be eminently suitable, but are seldom small enough. Within reason the larger the card the better, but compasses designed for large vessels will be too heavy and in other respects not really suitable for small boats.

If a compass is removable for stowage, you should take care to lock it firmly into position when shipping it for use.

Compass error

The principal source of compass error is the influence of ferrous metal aboard. Error caused by the presence of such static objects as an iron keel, inboard motor and so on are constant and can be taken into account for navigation once you have carried out an operation known as 'swinging the compass'.

The boat is accurately headed along either a bearing line or line of transits taken from the chart. Any difference observable between the compass reading and the bearing (expressed in Magnetic terms) is known as *deviation*. By putting the boat on to different headings, ideally at intervals of 30°, the deviation can be found over 360°. From the figures obtained a table or graph can be prepared as follows:

Heading in °(M)	Compass reading in °(C)	*Difference
030	032	+2
060	060	0
090	088	−2
120	116½	−3½

150	146	−4
180	176½	−3½
210	207½	−2½
240	240	0
270	271½	+1½
300	303½	+3½
330	334	+4
360	003½	+3½

* Expressed as the amount in degrees by which the *compass* reading differs from the Magnetic. In simple terms, to get a course to steer we apply this difference, the deviation, to the Magnetic course to get the answer.

A table for use aboard, once the above information has been obtained, is better set out in the following form. If you preface the figures with the suggested text, there will be no likelihood of confusion—*to get a course to steer apply the correction shown to the magnetic course concerned.*

Magnetic course	Correction
030	+2
060	0
090	−2
120	−3½
150	−4
180	−3½
210	−2½
240	0
270	+1½
300	+3½
330	+4
360	+3½

In practice it is all right to use a whole degree for correction. No one is going to contend that he can steer a small boat to within a half degree even if his compass card reads down to that, which is improbable. Sensible interpolation should be used for courses within the 30° intervals. And obviously, if you wish to convert compass course to Magnetic for any reason, simply apply the

deviation to the compass course with the sign reversed, eg 032°
(C) = 032 — 2 = 030° (M).

Some navigators prefer to use a graph which helps in
interpolation. One can be constructed using the original table,
as illustrated below (Fig 41); it should be prefaced by the following caption for easy use—*for a course to steer apply the correction
abreast the magnetic course concerned.*

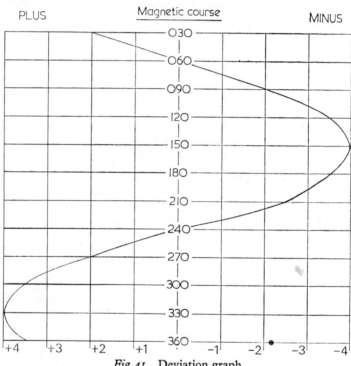

Fig 41 Deviation graph

Other methods of swinging can be used, and one convenient
for a small boat involves the use of a handbearing compass. If
this is kept away from rigging, lifelines and other metallic
influences, it can be assumed to be error-free and its reading
compared with that of the steering compass on the requisite
headings. It can be taken out in the tender and lined up with the

fore and aft line of the parent boat from astern, when a direct comparison can be made. Alternatively it can be held in the bows of the yacht and accurately lined up from fore to aft, in which case its reading will need 180° reciprocal correction.

When swinging, as accurate a course as possible must be sailed, and this brings out an interesting point which is relevant to steering at all times, particularly when trying to fetch a mark. If a helmsman sits off the centreline of the boat, which is almost always, he may tend to keep the stemhead in line with the mark, whereas to sail the boat correctly along its heading his line of sight should parallel the fore and aft line. For purposes of swinging it is convenient to stick a strip of black tape on top of the coach roof, accurately aligned fore and aft.

Compass adjusting

On some boats, particularly those with steel hulls, deviation is gross and needs to be eliminated or at least minimised. This is a task known as compass adjusting and is best done by a specialist. It entails the manipulation of subsidiary magnets set in or around the body of the compass. If your deviation amounts to no more than about 5° on any heading, allow for it in the deviation table and don't worry further. Refrain from tampering with any adjusting magnets fitted, apart from sealing them against rust, which may alter their characteristics, and protecting them against accidental movement.

Siting the steering compass

It is vital that the helmsman has a direct view of the card and lubberline, or grid, at all times. An oblique view will cause errors of parallax and cause the wrong course to be followed. If your chosen siting reveals unacceptable deviation, see if it can be remedied by changing the stowage of movable iron—say by shifting an outboard from a cockpit locker. If this proves impossible, you will either have to have the compass adjusted or move it to another site.

Fig 42   Line of sight when steering. Helmsman's line of sight (x)
and boat's heading (y)

Variable errors

If your engine is sited near the compass, it can exert a different attraction when running, owing to fields created by electric circuits. Although diesels have no ignition, they may still drive dynamos or alternators. If this situation has to be accepted, it may call for the use of a separate deviation chart when the motor is running.

Metal carried by the crew or left lying around the steering position, like knives and spikes or winch handles, can cause unsuspected errors. *Your crew needs constant reminding about this.* It is a real source of possible hazard, and the following cautionary tale is true.

I once carried a comparative stranger on a passage race. Each time he took the helm there seemed to be a windshift and after some hours we were well off course. After hours of worry I ran down the cause of our troubles. Having repeatedly assured me that he carried no ferrous metal on him, in proof he eventually produced, from the kangaroo pocket of his oilies, the only bit of metal about him. It was brass, he said. And so it was. A sizeable, highly polished, and obviously cherished *brass compass*!

Food cans can be magnetised during processing and the food locker is best not located near the compass. Loudspeakers of portable radios are pernicious and must be kept at least 6ft away from a compass. Young pop fans leave them all over the place. Other electrical gear needs watching out for, and even an innocent-looking torch may have a metal-clad battery. Pairs of wires should be closely twisted together to prevent the formation of a magnetic field when current passes through them.

Handbearing compass
A handbearing compass should fit the hand comfortably and be illuminated for night work. Sighting is made through an aperture under or over a prism which allows the card to be read simultaneously. More esoteric models occasionally appear, but it is questionable whether they have much advantage over the traditional and well proven types. Some portable RDF sets are equipped with a reliable and well lighted compass which can be used in a dual role, thus saving cash.

It pays to try to find a position aboard free from deviational influences in which to use the compass. If, exceptionally, this proves impossible, a set position should be adopted and a deviation chart prepared for the handbearing compass.

There is a knack in taking bearing from a small boat in a seaway. The user must be firmly braced, but able to flex from the waist in order to keep the observed object centred steadily for long enough to read the card. In transferring from one object to another, take care not to rotate the compass too rapidly or the card will oscillate and take time to settle. Unless the compass is kept roughly horizontal the card may rub or stick on the glass and give a false reading. At least two bearings should be taken of any object. If the results are not close, more should be taken until a reliable result or a realistic average is obtained. In small craft very often the best position is with your head sticking out of the companionway. Watch out for the proximity of metal booms, rigging and the steering compass.

Patent log
A means of measuring distance made good is essential for passage-making, and can be in the form of a mechanical or electronic log. Once calibrated, the old trusty Walker log is extremely robust and reliable. You only need to lubricate it frequently, and take in line and rotator in shoal water and when there is no way on the boat.

Mechanical models that employ a cable to transmit data from rotor or propeller to the display head suffer from friction in the cable, which may vary. Their small rotors or prods are liable to fouling from small weed and stuff which the Walker would shrug off.

Electronic gear can be very expensive and, apart from the manual clearance of the rotor, is probably impossible to repair aboard in the event of malfunction.

By watching your wake, experience will ultimately enable you to estimate the speed of your boat to within a quarter of a knot. However, there are elementary means of measuring speed for conversion into distance, such as the 'floating chip' (see p 19), the Dutchman's Log and so on. They can be used in emergency, but it is not really satisfactory to expect them to take the place of a reliable and accurate log if you want to navigate efficiently.

Lead and line
Echo sounders are useful aids to navigation and tell you how much water lies beneath the transducer. In deep water this is

largely of academic interest, despite all that is said about being able to use a line of soundings for navigation—a very tedious and dodgy job even in good conditions. In shoal water, where the hazards mostly lie, a leadline can be put to use with telling effect. Not only does it give the depth of water, but, if the bottom of the lead is hollowed out and filled with plasticine or candle wax, will reveal what sort of ground it is. The lead should weigh not less than 4lb, though 7lb is better, and the line must be prestretched. There is a traditional way of marking a line, but one knot tied in for each fathom interval can be seen by day and felt by night. All boats should carry lead and line.

Ancillaries

Good quality 6 × 50, 7 × 50 or 8 × 50 binoculars are essential for picking up and identifying marks and other objects. Good ones can be subjected to quite hard wear, but the prisms in cheap ones may easily be displaced by a slight knock. Even if this does not make them completely useless, an imperceptible maladjustment can give you a nasty headache in a short space of time. Buy as good a pair as you can afford from a reputable manufacturer. If you take care not to scratch the lenses, they will last a lifetime.

A radio direction finder (RDF set) is an aid to navigation which you should carry if possible. These sets have limitations and should not be used as a primary means of navigating, but their assistance in thick weather is comforting. They provide checks and confirmations of plotting in bad visibility and can be used, as will be explained, in getting fixes which would otherwise be unobtainable. In most cases even a slightly doubtful fix is better than none at all and an ever-increasing area of probable position.

A stop watch is useful for timing lights and, if you are inveigled into club racing, essential to a good start over the line. When using radio beacons, which transmit at fixed intervals, a stopwatch will help you to listen in at the correct times.

An alarm clock, best screwed down below in the dry, will

wake you in time to take advantage of tides when afloat and opening hours when ashore!

Meteorology is a wide, complex and not yet completely mastered subject, but a wise skipper will read as much as he can about it before undertaking long passages. It is not hard to learn to understand the inferences drawn from the movements of a barometer, and one should form part of the equipment of every boat.

Other equipment exists, irresistible to the man who wishes to get the last tenth of a knot out of his boat, but what has been detailed will suffice admirably for the average cruising skipper.

PLANNING A PASSAGE

Time spent in calm methodical planning for a passage will never be wasted. At sea there is always more than enough to do, and it is helpful to have all essential knowledge extracted and noted down before departure. Conscientious planning enables a start to be made at the correct time with a clear intention in mind. How far it can be adhered to will become apparent as you read on, but to depart with only a vague idea of how and when you might fetch your destination is unlikely to result in a happy and uneventful passage. To leave matters to be worked out in what might turn into bad conditions can be foolhardy, even dangerous, especially for the family man who has boat handling in addition to occupy his time.

A straightforward passage from Weymouth to Yarmouth (IOW) is used for illustration, and the general picture is shown in Fig 43.

In considering any passage it must be accepted that intervening conditions may force a skipper to alter his original plan. This will have immediate repercussions on the navigator, whose planning must therefore be flexible enough to allow for contingencies.

Charts
Assuming that all other equipment is aboard, small-scale charts

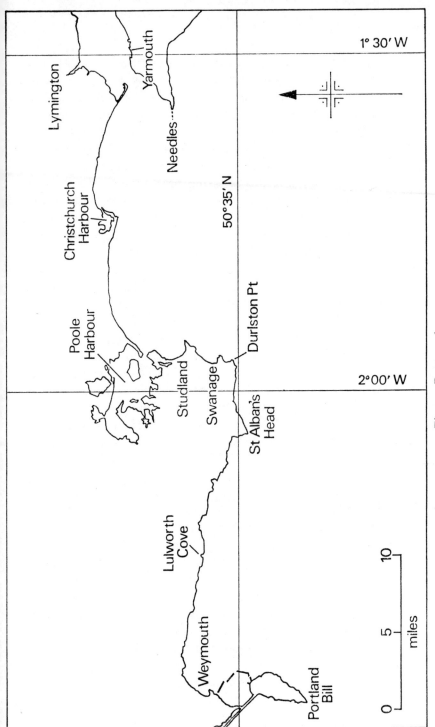

Fig 43 Passage chart

are selected to cover the waters from Weymouth to Yarmouth and, as a precaution, those covering Lyme Bay and the Solent. Harbour charts will be needed, not only for Yarmouth, but others on the way—Poole, Christchurch and Weymouth itself— and a 'pilot' with plans of the anchorages at Lulworth Cove, Swanage and Studland Bay. If refuges and anchorages in Lyme Bay and the Solent are also covered, so much the better.

Do not think that this is taking precaution to the limit of reason. It is far from uncommon for boats to be forced badly off course. To find yourself in an area for which you have no charts is dangerous, so it is sensible to cover areas contiguous to your immediate passage. As your cruising range extends, they will eventually be taken into use anyway, and the expenditure of a few shillings on extra charts is worthwhile insurance.

Directly between Weymouth and the Needles lies St Alban's Head, where the chart shows the existence of a race and overfalls. 'Pilots' will state that it is possible to pass close inshore at certain times of tide to avoid the worst of the race. At other times it is necessary to make an offing of 5 miles, except in very light conditions. A skipper will decide which course to take in the light of weather prevailing at time of departure, so we draw a line on the chart from just outside Weymouth harbour to just off the headland and another from Weymouth to 5 miles off the headland.

Research

Close scrutiny reveals that there are no underwater dangers along these courselines; water is deep and unobstructed for some distance on either side of them. However, the 'pilot' mentions the Lulworth Gunnery Ranges, which fire over a wide area of Weymouth Bay. The limits may not be marked on your charts and should be pencilled in. Enquiry at Weymouth Customs House discloses that the ranges are closed for the period of our passage, but under other circumstances it might have been necessary to stand well out to sea to avoid involvement. Many such hindrances to navigation exist and, as charts do not necessarily have them all marked in, a study of all available information in 'pilots' and elsewhere is a prerequisite to planning a passage.

Adverse winds

The ideal passage would be sailed on a broad reach under maximum spread of canvas and at full speed, but if our objective lies to windward, we shall be faced with consequential problems of navigation. Under such conditions a coastal sailor might find himself some way offshore, where fixes are unobtainable and accurate dead reckoning essential. The planned courseline degenerates into a baseline from which the track diverges some 50° or so as the boat tacks from one side of it to the other. A tack can be intrinsically advantageous or not, or it can be chosen deliberately for tactical reasons, such as anticipating a windshift.

Leebowing

In Fig 44 a boat is making toward an objective directly upwind and there is a tidal stream across the courseline. In choosing tacks it is generally desirable to use the one which will keep the boat nearest to its objective. It will be seen that this is the one which keeps the stream on the lee bow. It pays to stay on a favourable tack until it positively has become unfavourable. A temporary windshift may often make this appear so, but there is no point in changing tacks until you are certain that a fresh slant has been established. Folk who have been brought up on dinghies often tend to tack too early and too often. In the example, assuming the wind is constant, you can stay on the leebowing tack until you reach point X, when the opposite tack becomes more favourable and will allow you to reach your objective on one leg.

It is easy to get bemused by the benefits of leebowing. If the wind is not coming directly from the objective, it could be that more benefit would be obtained by taking the stream on the weather bow, and you can find this out by resolving vectors to see what track and speed can be made good on each tack. In doing so remember that the apparent wind will usually be stronger when you are leebowing, and this can produce very different speeds on the different tacks in light conditions.

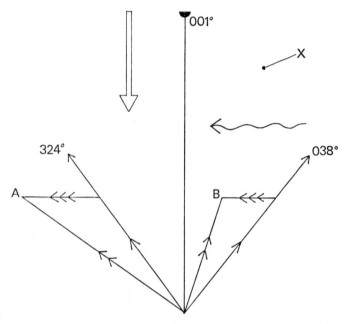

Fig 44   Leebowing advantage

A Weatherbowing position after 1hr
B Leebowing position after the same hour

Long and short tacking
Tacking not only takes time and effort, but can give rise to error by complicating dead reckoning so, on balance, long tacks are beneficial to the cruising man. The question of whether to tack long or short arises when one is travelling along a coastline with which streams normally roughly parallel (Fig 45). They run and turn earlier inshore than out in the channel. So, if you are headed into the stream, it will be advantageous to sail a long leg outward until after mid-tide, and only then tack to

arrive inshore to meet the slackening and then reversing stream. From then on a series of short tacks would keep you in a following stream until the time arrived to head offshore again and repeat the process.

Snags

If you are close in to a lee shore and hard on the wind, a breeze which suddenly shifts inland will force you to tack out to sea immediately. A high coastline might blanket it and leave you becalmed or even cause downdraught eddies blowing directly onshore. Beware of finding yourself in such a situation if coasting close in.

Some helmsmen are not very good at steering on the wind. Unless constantly watched, a careless man may sail by the luff for considerable periods. An experienced man is more likely to be prone to this than a novice who cannot use his sails to stay on the wind. If the breeze creeps round during such a period, the track made good may be well off the intended one.

When tacking inshore in thick conditions, full use should be made of soundings on the inward legs as an indication of shoaling. If a navigator becomes even slightly doubtful of his position at such a time, he must say so and let the skipper think about the advisability of anchoring or clearing out.

Setting a course to steer

On our passage to St Alban's Head, from which we have drifted slightly away, assume for simplicity that the wind is free and tacking complications absent. Let us decide to take the inshore course; it is necessary to know what to set on the compass.

Move your rule parallel to the courseline until it is centred over the nearest chart rose, whose perimeter it will cut at two points. Take the one corresponding to the proposed direction of travel; you will by now have made up your mind whether to use True or Magnetic degrees for the purpose.

If tidal streams are going to set in any way athwart the course-

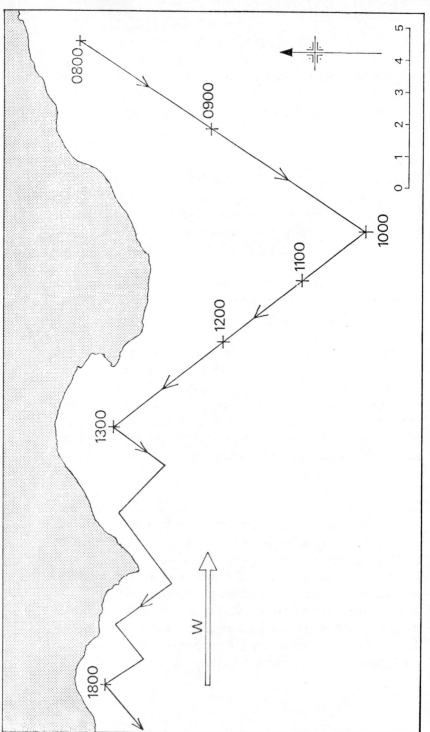

Fig 45 Long and short tacking. Set of streams offshore and inshore at 1000 is easterly. Streams change inshore at 1200 and 1000,

line, they will force the boat to travel at an angle to her heading. Before we can compute a course to steer, we must calculate the effect of the stream.

Tidal streams
The use of tidal stream atlases may be found a bit difficult at first due to their small scale, but practice and perseverance will bring familiarity with their shortcomings. Most yachtsmen's guides give more detailed drawings of streams, on a larger scale, and it is better to use them if available. Best of all is the use of a diamond on the chart if one lies near your position. In using diamonds remember that the printed table referring to them will be in True degrees, and need conversion.

Atlases should be prepared for use during the planning period by lightly pencilling important times during the proposed passage in the margins of corresponding pages. HW Dover for our chosen day is at 0230 and 1515, so that on the page showing the state of streams 3hr after HWD will appear the pencilling 0530; on the next page showing 4hr after HWD will appear 0630 and so on. Also, the interpolatory rate scale can be pencilled with a line representing the mean Dover tide range for the day.

An assumption will have to be made initially about the speed you will be making through the water under anticipated conditions. If this turns out to be erroneous, it will be possible to make course corrections, as explained later.

Take any point on your proposed courseline, ie the line from Weymouth harbour to close in St Alban's Head, and mark it A. From A draw the stream vector taken from your atlas to terminate at B. The length AB is made proportional to the rate of stream— say 1in to 1kn. On the same scale set your pencil compasses to a length to represent your assumed boat speed—say 5in for 5kn. With B as centre describe a small arc to cut the courseline at C. The result will look something like Fig 46.

In order to make good the track AC you will have to sail in the direction BC, which can be laid off a chart rose or grid. Of course, you will actually start sailing from A and your course will follow the dotted line, not BC.

The distance made good in the hour concerned will be proportional to the length AC. If the figure is stated in miles, it represents the speed made good over the ground (along the track), for it

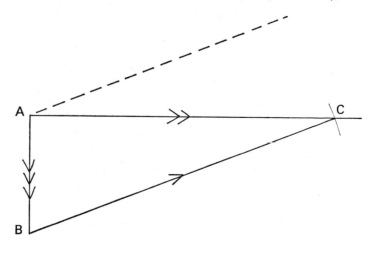

Fig 46   Allowance for tidal stream

will be seen that any number of nautical miles sailed in 1hr will have been at the same number of knots, because by definition 1kn = 1nm per hour.

Distances on a chart are picked off with dividers and laid off against the scales along the *sides*, roughly abreast of the line being measured. These are the latitude scales and fairly accurately represent distance measured on the face of the chart. The ones appearing at top and bottom edges are longitude scales, which have been distorted for cartographical reasons. They are not used for measuring distance, but only for purposes of correspondence when transferring information from one chart to another, or for quoting a position.

Two things remain. To correct the Magnetic course BC for

deviation and to find out how long it will take to reach St Alban's Head, so that you can give an estimated time of arrival (ETA).

Deviation

The magnetic course will be somewhere about 100° (M), and if there were no deviation on that heading you could tell the helmsman to steer 100° (C). However, if deviation is shown on the deviation table or graph to exist for a heading of 100° (M), it should be added or subtracted as appropriate to find the course to steer.

ETA

You have determined the distance AC, which is how far you will have travelled in the first hour. By then calculating the various rates and sets of stream for succeeding hours, you will discover how long it will take to cover the distance along the whole of the first leg. Assume it to be 4hr.

On our chosen day this means leaving at 0500 to arrive at 0900, the time of LW Dover. Being averse to early rising, we wonder if there would be any advantage in departing with the start of the flood at 0900; over the full period of the tide the stream will average 1½kn. In this way we could make 6½kn over the ground, amounting to 39nm by 1500. This would surely fetch us into Yarmouth.

Measurement of the complete courseline confirms that this is the distance to be covered and, on the face of things, the entire passage could be made on one tide. It would necessitate taking the passage outside the race, as the inshore one would not be feasible at our new ETA of 1130 off St Alban's. However, nothing has been allowed for as a margin of error, and we have already made one, overlooking the fact that the outside course is something over a mile longer. Delay for any reason—and at sea there are plenty—would find us punching an ebb as it streamed out of Hurst Narrows and down the Needles channel, doubtless kicking up a fuss of wind against tide. This can be a wet and disheartening task, and it would obviously be better to start earlier, head the slower stream in Weymouth Bay, take the shorter passage inshore and wind up with stream and breeze in our favour at the end of the passage.

Two lessons emerge. It is essential to study a passage *right through* from departure to arrival before coming to any decision about course and time of departure. Secondly, always pay full regard to tidal streams when you are coasting. They can lift you wonderfully on your way or prove a dismal drag. The wise mariner does not waste his time butting against a tide, during the period of which a remarkably short distance may be covered. Instead he lies asleep or fishing until they turn to his advantage. If there is a third lesson here, it is that a margin of time should be allowed for possible adverse conditions. In tidal waters this more often means a flat calm than a gale of wind.

Further action

ETA St Alban's has been calculated and similar working will show ETA Yarmouth. You can then reliably tell your skipper on the evening before departure: 'If the weather turns out as forecast, which seems probable, we should leave at 0500 and steer 097° (C). This will bring us inside St Alban's race at 0900 when streams will be slack; I'll give you a fresh course to follow then. We should arrive off Yarmouth approximately 1330'.

More work remains before the navigator can get his head down. He ought to prepare lists of buoys and other marks to be met with, lists and characteristics of lights and sound signals, and beacon frequencies within range. Above all he will plan for the unpredictable, notably adverse weather conditions.

For example, should the wind increase considerably during the first leg, it might be advisable to clear outside the race to avoid closing a tricky lee shore. In this case note must be made of the extent of the race itself and any buoys to be encountered on a fresh course. Once past Durlston Point the skipper might decide to make for Swanage, Studland or Poole. He might stand on, but decide to take the channel N of the Shingles bank. Courses should be known in advance for such contingencies, which would entail further study, noting such things as the small races off Peveril Point and Old Harry, Poole bar, Christchurch ledge, more markers, depths of water at available anchorages and the changing effect of tidal streams and wind direction as courses are altered.

When crossing Weymouth Bay, you may notice the tendency of the stream to follow the coastline and set you inshore of your intended track. Such an effect is significant around large bays and often causes the unwary to become embayed—set so close inshore that the distant headland cannot be cleared easily. This situation needs to be kept in mind in bad visibility, and continuous employment of depth-sounding is a necessary precaution.

ON PASSAGE

Departure routines
The planned courseline becomes obsolete once your boat is set on course, and the first leg should be erased from the chart. From now on until St Alban's running information will be marked in, and this will seldom coincide with the planned track. Too many lines close together are confusing.

Routine for getting on course is a fairly standard practice to which you will become accustomed. A suitable 'point of departure' is chosen, such as a convenient buoy off the harbour mouth or an arbitrary fix marked down on the chart (see pp 129–36). The more positive your PD the better will be the information gained from your first plot, so departure from the vicinity of a physical object is to be preferred. On getting the PD abeam, the log is streamed (put into operation) after being reset to zero; if it is not resettable, the reading should be noted. Reading and time should be written in against the PD; on short passages the date is not needed. Mark the PD as a fix and extend a line from that point in the direction of the course being steered. This should be marked in °(T) or °(M) according to your method of working.

The compass course is written alongside for easy reference. Your chart should now show something like Fig 47.

Abeam bearings
It is worth pointing out here that an abeam bearing needs consideration. If you say that something 'is abeam', it means

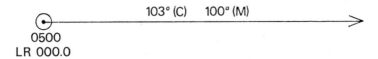

103° (C)   100° (M)

0500
LR 000.0

Fig 47   Plotting entry

that it lies at 90° to your *heading*, ie athwartships. This is not the same thing, by any means, as lying at 90° to your *track*. Later on, in considering the angular difference between heading and track, you will sometimes encounter a situation as shown in Fig 48. If you alter course when your chosen mark is 'abeam' instead

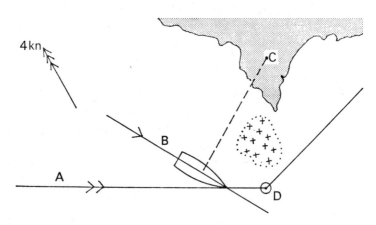

Fig 48   Abeam bearings

A Track   C Shore mark
B Heading   D Intended point of altering course

of at 90° to your track, you will be unable to clear the danger. Thus, if leaving instructions with a helmsman, you would tell

118

him to alter course when the mark bore so many degrees from the boat, and not just say 'when it is abeam'.

Logbook

All running information should now be entered into a logbook, which is a record of a boat's achievements. It is usual to keep a rough log for use on passage and later transcribe the entries into a Ship's Log. Printed logbooks can be bought for such permanent record and a 'Chinese' copy of them made for rough work. Not only navigational data is entered but notes of weather, sail carried and its changes, passing vessels and many other matters of nautical use and significance. Very often you can check back on a doubtful position from log entries. If insurance claims arise, your logbook can be valuable evidence, and it is altogether sensible to maintain such a record. A well written log is nice for nostalgic mulling over during dreary winters. The first entry for our passage could read something like this:

> 7 Jul 75. 0445 cleared Weymouth harbour. 0500 streamed log off DG buoy 50° 36′ N: 2° 25′ W. Log reading 245.3nm. Course 095° (097° (C)). Wind SW3. Sea smooth; light swell. Warm and sunny, 2/10ths cloud. Reaching under main and genoa.

Dead reckoning

A position should be marked on the plot at regular intervals of not more than 1hr. In bad visibility or close to shore or dangers you may find it better to plot more frequently so that your position is known to closer limits. To find your position, first read the log and note the time; distance made *through the water* is found by subtracting the previous reading. This distance should be picked off with dividers from the latitude scale abreast the position. This distance is stepped off along the courseline from the PD and marked in as DR, together with a note of log reading and time (Fig 49). This point, the dead reckoning position (DR), is not necessarily your actual position and has to be corrected for the effects, among other things, of tidal streams. Your DR position has now to be transferred carefully from chart to tidal atlas on the page corresponding to the time of plot. This is done by

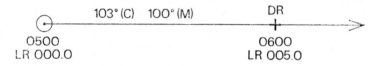

Fig 49 Dead reckoning

using the latitude and longitude scales in the margins of both chart and atlas. Where you find your DR then lying somewhere between stream data positions, which is almost always, an approximation has to be made and you must be precise in transferring the DR and accurate in interpolation. With experience you will get reliable figures, although it may seem hard to start with.

Correction to DR
Draw a line on the chart from the DR position in the direction of the set of stream and step off a length representing its rate in knots and fractions of a knot. This will be the distance the boat has moved under the effect of the stream in the elapsed hour. Intervals of longer or shorter than 1hr between plots will mean calculation to find the set during the period, which is one good reason for sticking to hourly plotting.

Against the measured length mark △ and give the line three arrows for tidal stream. Join ⊙ and △ . Mark this line with two arrows for track (Fig 50). When laid off against the chart rose, it gives the direction of track, and its length is proportional to the distance made good (*over the ground*) during the hour in question. Stated in knots it is the speed made good.

Estimated position

The point △ is your estimated position (EP) at the time the log was read, although you will be a little way past it by now, and your chart should look like Fig 50. Contrast this with Fig 46, where speed and distance made good were being estimated from an assumed boat speed. Here you are determining actual figures achieved.

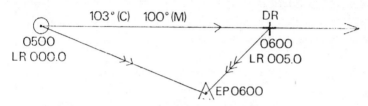

Fig 50 Estimated position

Leeway

Many books will now say that a correction to your EP should be made for leeway, which is expressed as the number of degrees the boat has been moved off track by the effect of the breeze. With suitable deference to those more knowledgeable about such things, I say ignore it for coastal passages.

A decent modern cruiser will make little leeway and that only when hard on the wind. At most it might amount to about 2°, which means being 5 cables off track after a 15 mile passage, during which there will have no doubt been the opportunity to take several fixes. These will have shown up errors in track, including any small leeway. It is a difficult quantity to estimate, being individual to a boat, and only years of experience with a boat will enable you to say 'on this course, under these conditions, I shall make $1\frac{1}{2}°$ of leeway'. Wind which will create enough leeway to mention will be strong enough to raise seas whose effect on a boat's progress is far more pronounced.

Checking the plot
Every effort must be made to establish the validity of an EP, and you should confirm your calculated position by means of a fix whenever possible. If a difference exists, the fix should be repeated until it can be relied upon and adopted as the base for continuing the plot.

Differences shown up must always be satisfactorily explained away. Inaccuracies in the plot can result from many causes, notably arithmetical error, compass error, log error, bad helming and unpredicted variations in rate of stream. It is improbable that the set of a stream will vary greatly, but both its set and rate can be seriously affected by surface currents caused by a wind blowing for an appreciable time in a constant direction. The effect of a surface current is greatly dependent upon a boat's draught: the deeper the keel the less the effect.

Log error should not occur once the instrument has been calibrated, unless the rotor fouls. This can easily be checked and rectified.

The steering compass can be checked for error against the handbearing one. Any discrepancy calls for a search for the cause, such as movable iron.

Arithmetical error will be shown up if a careful check of working is made. It pays where possible for another person to work out the sums independently for purposes of comparison.

Unless watched, some helmsmen are inattentive to the compass; a wise skipper will always watch for this and gently chide an offender. Often a man steers a bad course from inability to anticipate the swing of a boat in a seaway, usually when the wind is aft. There may be fear of a sudden gybe, which causes a tendency to head into the wind. Others, when on the wind, luff up every time there is a gust and this results in a noticeable tracking up to weather; more than enough, incidentally, to offset any possible leeway. These, and other errors made often by quite 'salted' helmsmen, need to be thought about when you are looking at errors in the plot. It is difficult to think of a case where bad helming would result in a downwind drift, and if you consistently find yourself upwind of your EP, pay careful attention to your helmsmen.

Once such sources of error have been tracked down and nullified, all that is left to account for further error is the stream effect. This will have to be calculated and a fresh course steered to take it into account, as follows. Reliable fixes are used to start and to end a run. As log and compass errors, and so on, have all been checked and eliminated, the DR at the end of the run can be assumed as accurate. The second fix will be your EP, obviously, and a vector triangle is completed about the three points Fix 1, Fix 2 and DR position. From this the rate and set of the stream experienced can be read off and used for further plots.

Offshore
On longer passages out of sight of land, where fixes are unobtainable by visual means, the effect of streams must be given careful attention. In the English Channel, for instance, streams run hard at ·springs and in a generally NE–SW direction. When crossing in search of the duty-free goods, you are going to be under the influence of these streams for 12hr or so, and must plot accurately if you wish to achieve a satisfactory landfall. If the effect of a flood, or ebb, is aggregated for its whole period, small fractional calculations can be avoided, as can frequent interpolations on the atlas. A little table can be written out, as follows:

Hour	Rate of stream	Set of stream
1	0·5kn	090°
2	1·1kn	095°
3	1·9kn	095°
4	2·0kn	090°
5	1·5kn	085°
6	1·0kn	075°
Drift	8·0nm	6/530
		Mean set 088°

Using this information and a vector of the distance through the water and mean course sailed, you may construct a triangle which will give the mean track sailed during the tide.

A commonly held fallacy is that a 12hr crossing of the Channel will result in streams cancelling out and that a direct course can be followed from point to point. This is not so, and if you happen to cross any stretch of sea from one coast to another, do not be tempted to make facile assumptions or indulge in wishful thinking. The facts are always there for you to use. Streams are quite a bit stronger as you approach France, and a downstream landfall might cause a considerable delay in fetching your objective. Heading should be reviewed at least once during the passage and always with a change of set. The question of leebowing tides has already been dealt with. Once land becomes visible, you can stand on your course until it is near enough for reliable fixes to be obtained, but low visibility calls for accurate positioning before closing an inhospitable coast.

RDF is a great comfort on a blind approach, but the mariner's best friend is his patent log at such a time. As soon as the distance run indicates the proximity of the coast, you can decide whether to stand in prudently, stand off until you can get more information, or even consider abandoning the approach for the time being. This is a seaman's decision, but can only intelligently be based on the reliability of navigation.

THE FIX

Buoys loom large in the life of a coastal navigator and to be close by a clearly marked and accurately stationed one provides an excellent fix. A lightship is better, for if it gets out of position, it notifies the fact to passing traffic. The Nab tower is better still. When closing any such object after a period without an accurate position, especially in low visibility, *make certain* that it is the one you are expecting (or hoping!) to see. Wishful thinking is only too often followed by careless observation, and to pick the wrong buoy out of a group bordering a danger could be fatal.

Buoys are regularly lifted for maintenance, and may or may not be replaced with a *locum tenens*. At times a buoy may be off station or have been moved to another position. Buoyage systems are in a state of continuous flux, especially in waters which are crowded with shipping. Information is promulgated in *Notices to Mariners* and you will be well advised to use them to correct your charts, almanacs and other sources of information.

Wreck buoys are laid as demanded and should be given a wide berth if unfamiliar. Their green lights are not always easy to discern and a good watch must be kept for them at night. The softness of the colour added to the fact that it customarily denotes safety on land makes it difficult to see why it was chosen for this vital marking.

Bearings
In light lists and almanacs bearings of lights and other fixed marks are given in *True degrees from seaward and measured clockwise*. Thus if you observe a light which is given as visible from 350° to 010°, you are necessarily to the southward of it. This convention is entirely logical, as bearings taken on a compass will, after correction, correspond.

Remember that bearings taken with a handbearing compass read Magnetic. When one is tired, it is too easy to forget that the bearing taken of a light just opening is not the same as its True bearing given on the chart.

Lights
It is useless to try to take the bearing of a light before it has been unmistakably identified, because wrong information can be more dangerous than no information at all. Confirming the periodicity of a light beyond doubt can be very troublesome in hard conditions, and a stopwatch should be used. Once again, avoid wishful thinking. Parts of a cycle can be obscured time and time again by wave crests and it helps to have your eye as far as possible above sealevel. Once the light is recognised, any little flash will

then help you to take its bearing. Lights are but pinpoints and hard to hold centred in the compass sights. It is best to keep both eyes open during periods of eclipse, with the compass held in front of the dominant eye. When the light reopens, it can more easily be brought central, and the idle eye then closed if wished.

Safety limits

A bearing, or series of bearings, can be used to good effect to keep you out of danger zones. Fig 51 shows a boat sailing into an anchorage bounded by reefs. A mark ashore, M, is chosen and lines MX and MY drawn on the chart clear of the reefs. As long

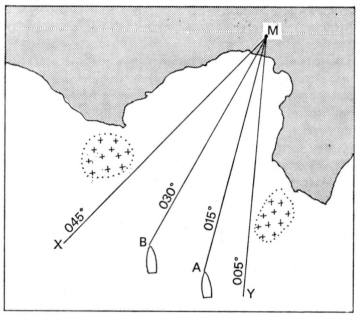

Fig 51 Danger limits

as the visual bearing of M stays between them it will be safe to stand on. If streams are taking the boat off track, it will become apparent immediately the bearing alters from, say, AM to BM. Heading can be changed to compensate for drift.

Astern bearings

It is often of assistance in determining stream effects if bearings are taken of an object astern. For example, in steering a course from the PD, should this be a fixed mark, a position line established at intervals will show the track being followed. Should this differ from the computed track, an adjustment will have to be made to the stream vector or course vector, whichever is found to be in error.

Converging tracks

Another use for repeated bearings is where tracks are converging—a situation which can be hazardous if a steamer is rapidly approaching a small boat. Fig 52 shows a typical case. As long as the relative bearing of ship and observer remains constant, there is a possibility of collision. Once the bearing opens, it means that tracks are no longer converging. Due to disparity in speeds. it is usual for the relative bearing to remain imperceptibly different for a considerable time, after which it opens increasingly rapidly. If it shows no signs of opening before the ship approaches to within about $\frac{1}{2}$ mile, the prudent sailor will take avoiding action.

Position lines

A line passing through two fixed objects is known as a *transit line*; it can be drawn on the chart and its bearing laid off. Quite frequently a transit line is found printed on a chart for purposes of clearing a danger, eg 'The spire of St John's church in line with the watertower leads clear of the Grabbies'. An observer seeing the two objects in transit knows that his boat lies somewhere on the line, which is then known as a *position line* (PL). Another sort of PL is one connecting the boat with an object of known position whose bearing can be taken with a compass. An RDF

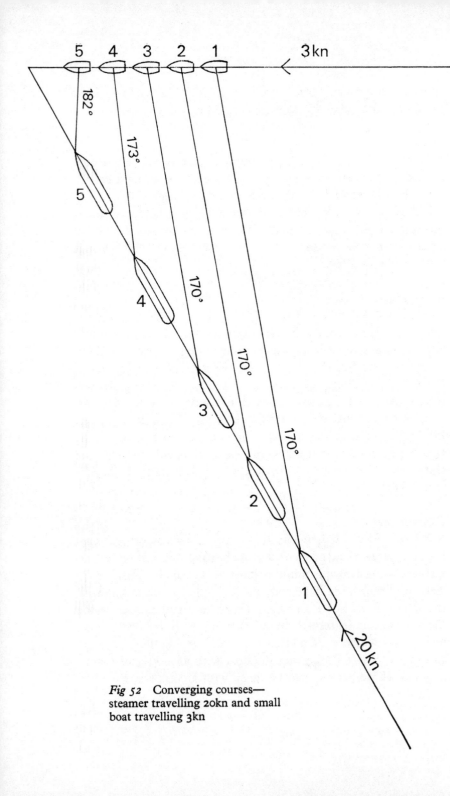

5 4 3 2 1   3 kn

182°

173°

170°

170°

170°

5

4

3

2

1

20 kn

Fig 52 Converging courses—
steamer travelling 20kn and small
boat travelling 3kn

bearing of a beacon is a PL. Such position lines form the basis of fixes, and in the following text both visual and radio beacons are treated as the same thing, although for navigation the limitations of RDF bearings must be noted. Fixes can be got from a combination of PLs obtained by any means.

Simultaneous fixes

A boat must lie, by definition, somewhere along its PL. If two PLs intersect, the boat must be positioned at the point of intersection. Plotting this position is known as taking a two-point (or two-line) fix (Fig 53). Its reliability depends on the accuracy of the bearings, the angle of cut and the care with which the lines are laid off. Bearings of distant objects are less reliable than those of closer ones and the optimum angle of intersection is 90°, so PLs should be selected accordingly if a choice exists.

Most radio beacons transmit on a 6-minute cycle, which may have to be waited out if a bearing is doubtful. During this time a boat can have travelled up to ½ mile or more, which means that a fresh bearing of a nearby beacon cannot be expected to be the same as the previous one. If a radio bearing is being combined with a visual sight, the latter should be taken last. If not, the boat may be some way off its visual PL by the time the radio bearing is established, particularly if it has to be repeated.

Three-point fix

A more reliable fix can be got by using three PLs, in which case the best angle of cut between each pair is 60°. The lines will almost never cut at the same point—suspect them if they do—but will form a triangle of error. Fig 54 shows that too small an angle of cut will result in an awkward triangle in which to estimate your position.

The closer to shore or hazard you find yourself, the smaller should be the acceptable area of doubtful position represented by the triangle. If one looks unreasonably large, the fix should be repeated.

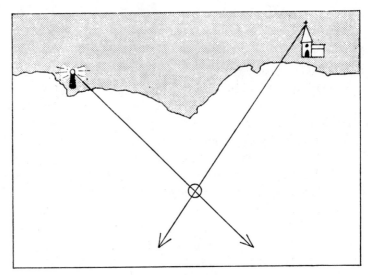

Fig 53   Two-point fix

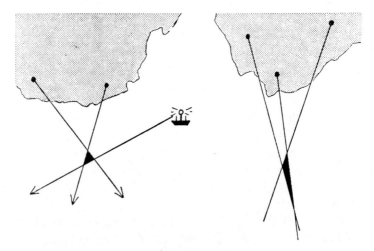

Fig 54   Three-point fixes. Note different sizes and shapes of shaded triangles

In open water there is little harm in continuing the plot from the centre of the triangle, but if there are dangers about, you should assume that you are taking a departure from that part of the triangle which is *most* dangerous. In Fig 55 it is clear that if you are at A, both tracks AB and AC will lead you clear of hazard. If you assume that you are at A and are in fact at X, the track XY is barely all right but XZ will put you right on the rocks.

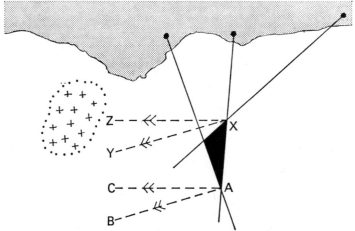

Fig 55 Triangle of error—tracks AB, AC and XY safe, track XZ dangerous

Transferred fixes

At times only a single mark will be available, but no opportunity should be lost to take its bearing, as it can be used to get a PL. This can be used later as the basis of a satisfactory fix, and there are various ways of going about the task.

In one, a PL is taken and transferred on the chart to intersect a second one taken from another mark met with later. The track during the intervening period is calculated by DR and laid off from the original PL. Fig 56 shows that it does not matter from which point on the first PL the track is drawn; no correction to DR position has been made, and through it a line is drawn parallel to the first PL. Where this intersects the second PL is the fixed position.

In Fig 57 DR has been corrected to give the EP at the time of

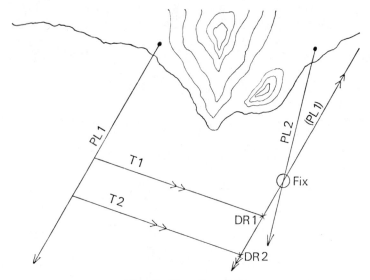

Fig 56   Transferred fix

fixing. It is obvious that the reliability of a transferred fix depends on the accuracy of your dead reckoning.

Running fix

A running fix is simply a transferred fix where the second PL is taken from the original mark, not a second one (Fig 58). The bigger the angle of cut between the PLs the better—it should ideally never be less than 30°—which means that considerable ground may have to be covered if speeds are slow or the mark is distant. Again, it depends on accurate dead reckoning for reliability.

Doubled angles

If you use the following method of getting a fix, or distance off,

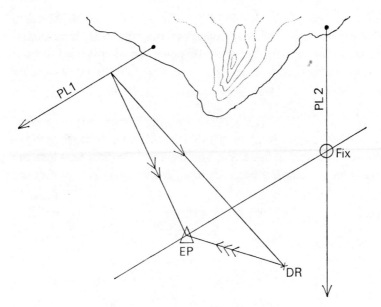

Fig 57 Transferred fix corrected

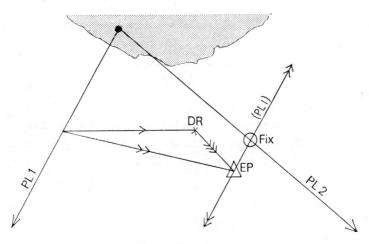

Fig 58 Running fix

133

a steady speed is desirable. The method is quite well suited to the requirements of the powerboat man but can have short-comings for the sailor. If the four-point variation is used to clear a headland by a certain distance, remember that streams accelerate and decelerate rapidly round headlands and their effect on the track of a slow boat can be significant.

In Fig 59 a boat is travelling along the track PR; at point P a relative bearing is taken of the mark M. This is angle MPQ—call it 30°. When the angle has increased to 60°, ie when the angle on the bow has been doubled, geometry will prove that the triangle MPQ is an isosceles and that the sides PQ and MQ are equal. This means that if you know the distance PQ, you have a bearing and distance fix when you are at M. PQ is, of course, got by means of dead reckoning.

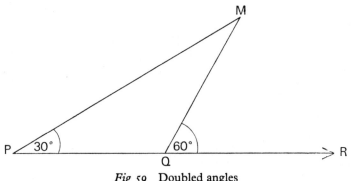

Fig 59   Doubled angles

Four-point fix

A special case is when the angle MPQ is 45°; MQR will then be 90° (Fig 60). In other words the mark will be abeam of the boat's *track*, and MQ will be the distance at rightangles to the mark. Go back to p 118 for the trap to be avoided when using this means of getting a distance off.

Dipping lights

Your position can be very accurately fixed if you know the bearing and distance of a mark—you merely step the distance off along the PL. The problem is, of course, to obtain an accurate distance.

There is a means of finding the distance of a light just visible above the horizon which is very useful when closing a coast from seaward. When planning to do this, say on a cross-Channel

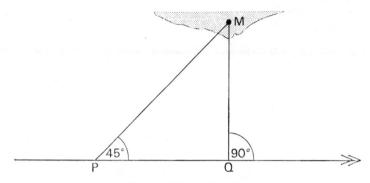

Fig 60 Four-point fix

passage, it pays to time your arrival to some 10–12 miles off the coast just before dawn. Lights then clearly visible will permit you to fix your position and make any necessary alterations to course. As the sun comes up, you will be approaching shore marks usable for visual fixes.

The range of lights is marked against them on the chart, but if they are weak, it is not necessarily their 'dipping distance' which should be confirmed. Almanacs give tables for reading off the distance of dipping lights, but you can calculate this for yourself by adding the results of the following two sums:

I   Distance in nm of horizon from observer's eye

———————————————————————

$1.15 \sqrt{\text{Height of eye in feet above WL}}$
and
II   Distance in nm of light behind horizon

———————————————————————

$1.15 \sqrt{\text{Height of light in feet (taken from chart)}}$

From any fixed position on board the height of eye will be a constant and should be committed to memory or noted on the gen-board. An eye 5ft above WL observing a light just on the horizon and at a height of 100ft will be $2·57 + 11·50 = 13·07$nm away from it.

In some cases the height may not be given on the chart, but only the range of visibility, which must then be used as the dipping distance. Dipping distances are quoted for a height of eye of 15ft and a correction has to be made as follows:

$$
\begin{aligned}
\text{Distance of horizon from } 15\text{ft} &= 4·45\text{nm} \\
\text{Distance of horizon from } 5\text{ft} &= 2·57\text{nm} \\
\hline
\text{Difference} &\;\; 1·88\text{nm}
\end{aligned}
$$

For basic navigation in a small boat it does to assume that a light will be observed at 2nm less than its given dipping distance.

Reasonable care must be taken in using dipping lights. Quite often a high light is obscured by cloud or mist, and the land picked up before the light is ever seen. Again, in a swell the observer must make sure that the light is actually dipping and not just bobbing up and down behind wave crests. It helps to get as high as possible, but this will vary the dipping distance.

When standing out to sea you can use an astern bearing of a dipping light to great advantage in checking your DR.

CHAPTER THREE

Harbour Lore

ANTICIPATION

As a boat nears harbour at the end of a passage, its crew will experience some degree of relief and a wish to relax which should be resisted for the moment. Oddly enough this is a time calling for a renewed effort of concentration. Offshore, there is time and space to spare, even if more or less crucial decisions have to be taken. Approach and entry to a strange harbour bring a welter of less vital matters than are met with on the main, but which nevertheless demand close and immediate attention. Forethought, imagination and meticulous preparation are needed if irritation and frustration are to be avoided.

Charts give bald facts, but there are well written guides and 'pilots' which are profusely illustrated with views of the approaches to and interiors of harbours. Admiralty and other 'pilots' give a mass of useful detail, although that is not expressly aimed at the yachtsman. Study of all this sort of information is beneficial, but none of it will indicate immediate conditions. Activity in and around harbours varies according to season and time of day. For example, moorings are laid and lifted, pontoons shifted about, and the weather plays a large part in setting the scene. You have to use imagination to put flesh on the factual skeleton.

Scale effects

The scale of charts, particularly harbour charts and those of their approaches, varies widely. Sketches on identically sized pages in a guidebook can represent an area ranging from a puddle like Mousehole to an inland sea like Poole Harbour. As your experi-

137

ence grows, you will be able to comprehend the effects of scale, but initially you will inevitably visualise incorrectly the amount of navigable water to be found. It is disorienting to find it much larger than imagined and disconcerting to find it smaller. Also, plans give little if any idea of the height of alongside and nearby buildings, their relative prominance or the fact that one may be almost completely masked by another. If you had intended to use such a hidden building as a mark after entry, you might be confused and a little lost.

The breeze can be seriously affected by such things as tall buildings along the quay or a steep-to entry channel. Any combination of lost breeze, adverse stream and nearby hazards could cause a minor crisis.

Water

There is seldom coincidence between tidal heights and tidal streams, so do not assume misguidedly that there will be no streams in and around harbours at high and low tide. This applies particularly to the mouths of rivers and to narrow estuaries.

The height of tide at time of entry is apparent from tide-tables, but the effect of different heights of water on the *appearance* of some harbours is astonishing. Although you may have correctly reasoned that certain parts of it will have dried out, it can absolutely shock you to see how little water really remains and how crammed it is with other craft. Conversely, at high water there may seem to be endless space for manoeuvre, whereas you will in practice be confined to narrow channels of navigable water. Quick identification of such channels may not be easy, especially at night. There is no substitute for experience, and if you happen to travel by land around your cruising area, a divergence from the beaten track to inspect harbours can pay dividends later. Committal to harbour needs to be the subject of careful research, thoughtful consideration and the formulation of alternative plans of action. This can all be carried out at the planning stage or during the passage, but one thing is sure. It must be done long before the harbour mouth opens, for then your mind and hands will be occupied with immediate matters.

The approach
Unless a harbour is quite open to the sea, and often when it is, you will need to identify a buoy or other mark as the lead-in to the approach. A couple of miles offshore there is frequently a great landfall buoy to be found. From this a course can be steered to join up with the channel markers leading on to the harbour. Intimate knowledge of the buoyage system is invaluable at such times.

Route card
If an approach is long, tortuous, fringed with hazards or otherwise complex, it helps to prepare pilotage notes in advance. These can conveniently take the form of a route card as depicted (Fig 61).

It is only necessary to note marks essential for conning the boat and the chart should be kept handy for taking note, or a bearing, of any other object if necessary for any reason. Distances, courses to steer and characteristics of marks and lights are marked conventionally on the card. Courses are preferably stated in °(C) so that a change of course needs no thinking about. If the route reads from the bottom up, as in Fig 61, it will be easy to follow the arrows, but this is a matter of personal preference.

It may be inadvisable to approach too close during twilight hours when night vision is not yet fully in operation. Harbour lights are very often hard to distinguish against a background of domestic and street lighting. If you cannot get in in decent light, a middle night approach might be planned for when most shore lights will be out.

In a tricky channel the leadline or echo sounder should be in constant use. As your time of arrival after a longish passage may not be precisely as estimated, it is better not to try to include

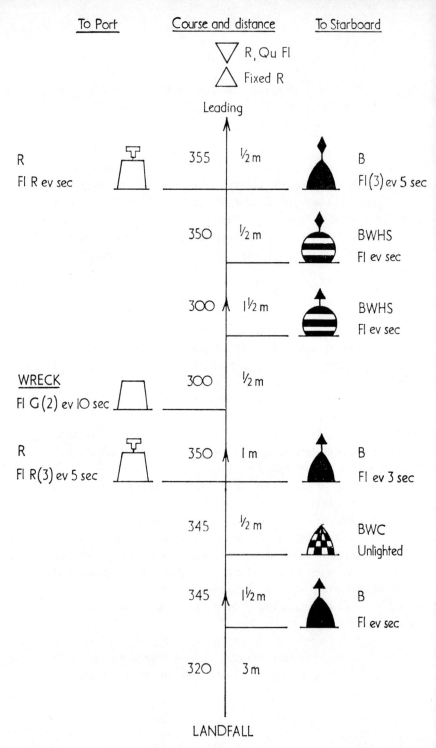

Fig 61 Pilotage route card

depths of water on the route card but to use chart soundings corrected for the height of tide at your time of arrival.

In thick weather and busy channels a bow lookout is advisable. His signals to the helmsman must be agreed in advance and be unmistakable in intention.

The Collision Rules must be closely followed in restricted waters, and this means sticking to the starboard side of a channel on most occasions. Ships have right-of-way in channels where they are not fully manoeuvrable, and there may or may not be enough water outside the channel markers for you to resort to at a pinch. Make sure, although in any case of emergency it will be better to risk a grounding than a collision with a big ship.

You will have to decide whether it is safe or sensible to use sail in a channel, and this must rest on weight and direction of wind, rate and set of streams, visibility and, not least, your own skill. The boat must be fully manoeuvrable. It would not be sensible, for instance, to tack up a busy channel into a headstream or to run under a press of wind over tide. Commonsense must be your salvation, but it is extraordinary how often one sees small craft in an indeterminate state of control arguing the toss with other vessels—even big ships. Shipmasters can be seriously embarrassed by such antics. Part and parcel of the business of seamanship is to care about the other chap at all times.

Cross streams are frequently found at harbour entrances, especially when these lead off a channel or river. 'Pilots' give notice of their existence, and they habitually cause eddies and disturbances around pierheads which call for caution and a wide berth. Some of them are really menacing at certain states of tide, eg Exmouth Dock.

One horror to beware of is a training wall. This is a mole, usually of rough or broken stone or rock, leading out seaward from the vicinity of a harbour and submerged at some states of tide. It is intended to prevent silting of the channel by directing the flow so that it will scour the fairway. Often you will observe a clearly visible and well marked pier or mole on one side of a channel, while not too distant on the opposite side is a submerged training wall. It should rightly be marked with beacons but as streams may flow across it, quite hard, after submersion, the marks are often adrift.

A similar danger, not necessarily beaconed, will also be found where the seaward end of a mole has been destroyed at some time and left, unrepaired and uncleared, to extend submerged some distance outward of the visible portion. Many such hazards resulted from wartime activities and can be found on the northern coast of France, eg Omonville or Braye—harbours regularly visited by British yachts.

Bars

Harbour bars are reputed to moan, but this sound will more likely be emitted by a sailor who attempts to cross one without due care and attention. Little damage will occur to a boat that brushes its keel in calm conditions, when the precise calculation of depth over the bar on a rising tide is not critical. Factors which cannot be disregarded include the height of any scend of sea and the existence of breakers: 4ft waves will have the effect of reducing the calculated depth of water by 2ft in a trough, and as their crests accelerate and topple in shoaling water, they will take a boat forward and downward with them. If she strikes or broaches, or both, the situation will be very dangerous. Several lifeboats have been lost through this cause, although, admittedly, the weather was far worse than you will be likely to meet with on short coastal passages.

Bars demand respect. Plenty of water must be allowed before crossing them in anything but benign conditions. If the time is wrong, you may have to heave-to, jill about in the offing or otherwise let time elapse until it is safe to cross. It is not generally realised that breakers may not be very obvious to seaward under certain circumstances, and only when over in safety will a worried sailor look astern and realise what had caused him so much unanticipated trouble.

Harbour regulations

Added to natural and manmade physical hazards are administrative ones connected with ports and harbours, such as signals which are displayed to control entry or exit. For instance, Dover is not the only harbour which requires that a positive request for entry or departure be answered by an affirmative signal before one can proceed. Such requirements must be ascertained in advance and correct procedures followed. Entry and departure may also be restricted to certain entrances and specific times. If you plan to enter an inner locked basin and do not confirm the times of opening and closing the gates, you may have a dreary time if the outer harbour is one that dries out.

Naval ports are controlled by a governmental authority and in the UK come under the jurisdiction of a Queen's Harbourmaster. Royal Dockyards are extensive in area, and their limits, which spread out into adjacent waters, are marked on charts. Special regulations applying to various Royal Dockyards are given as appendices to Admiralty 'pilots' and must be strictly complied with. They also prescribe that HM ships can display navigational lights and signals not to be found in Collision Rules.

Depth of water

In restricted waters, before anchoring and on many other occasions, you will need to know the depth of water in a given position at a certain time. The small figures scattered over the face of a chart are called soundings. When reading them, consult the scale of the chart carefully; soundings are usually given in fathoms on large-scale charts, but when you are using approach and harbour charts, the soundings may be given in feet. Once metrication of charts has become universal the problem will disappear, but this will be some considerable time in the future; all soundings will then be given in metres.

A sounding gives the depth of water at that point below an arbitrary level known as Chart Datum (CD). Small figures like soundings but which are underlined are called Drying Heights, and give the height of the ground above CD at the point concerned. Now, we need not concern ourselves with the technicalities attaching to fixing of a Chart Datum and need only remember that *depth of water* is defined as either *height plus soundings* or *height minus drying height.*

If you care to use the information given in almanacs and other books, it is possible to find depths of water to the last inch. The following rule of thumb is probably of more use to the weekend sailor.

Extract three figures from your tidal information in the almanac —height of tide at HW, height of tide at LW, and mean level for your chosen position. If height LW is not given, as may happen for certain places, you find it by simply doubling the mean level and subtracting the height HW. These heights are given in relation to the relevant CD.

The difference between the heights of HW and LW is known as the *range* of the tide. Divide the range by twelve and call the resulting figure a unit. The level of water will range from high to low in roughly 6hr and back again to high in the succeeding 6. During each 6hr period it will follow this progression of units per hour:

$$1-2-3-3-2-1$$

Given the time of high (or low) water, it is a simple thing to find the depth of water at any time.

Example

Height of HW (at 0300)		18ft
Height of succeeding LW		3ft
	Range	15ft

A unit is therefore $\dfrac{15\text{ft}}{12} = 1\frac{1}{4}\text{ft}$ or 15in.

Needed to find the depth of water at 0700.

This is 4hr after HW, so the tide will have decreased in height by $1 + 2 + 3 + 3 = 9$ units or $11\frac{1}{4}$ft, putting it at $18 - 11\frac{1}{4} = 6\frac{3}{4}$ft above CD. The depth of water at that time is the sum of height plus the sounding at your position, say:

Height of tide at 0700	$6\frac{3}{4}$ft
Sounding	2ft
Depth of water	$8\frac{3}{4}$ft

If your boat draws 4ft 9in, there will be 4ft under your keel at 0700. In another 2hr, at LW, the depth will only be $3 + 2 = 5$ft —mighty close to the base of your keel. The moral is that when anchoring or tying up for any length of time you should calculate the depth of water available to you during the entire period.

PREPARATION FOR ENTRY

You can expect harbours to be crowded, so do not assume that a berth chosen on paper will be empty when you arrive. Instead of the comfortable alongside berth envisaged, you may have to accept a mooring, or even an anchorage, in a more inconvenient spot.

Full manoeuvrability is essential and this dictates that except in large open-water harbours the auxiliary must be used. Unless unduly strong streams exist, an outboard is adequate, for it is surprising how little power is needed to push a boat along at harbour speeds. It is more convenient to have one fitted with forward, neutral and reverse, but this is not by any means essential.

You should be able to stop if needs be, and this means keeping an anchor ready to trip. A drogue, such as a bucket, will cut down excess way rapidly, but a prudent skipper ought to make his way around a harbour at very low speed and not have to resort to any such expedient. Warps and fenders should be unstowed and placed at salient points about the deck, and a boathook and heaving line made ready.

Fenders

A craft entering harbour should ready fenders for what will be her inboard side on tying up. Although proper fendering is essential to prevent damage to self and others, it is a subject which is often treated sketchily. Stowage must be found for enough *large* fenders to protect your craft; just because your boat is minuscule does not make it logical to carry tiny fenders. They have to provide sufficient clearance between your hull and its abutments to allow for rolling and surging. The minimum diameter of an effective fender is not less than 8in. They not only have to resist the weight of your boat, which may not be excessive, but that of heavier craft trying to grind her into a wall or against a trot of boats. Flimsy fenders will flatten or collapse under stress, so ensure that yours are man enough for their work.

Arriving alongside, the crew can move fenders about the side of the hull as required, and once you are made fast they can be belayed in their permanent positions. You are not likely to need more than three a side—four at the most—and if adjacent boats do their stuff it should not be necessary for you to carry a surplus of these bulky and irreducible objects. If you lie alongside a wall with projections like piles or buttresses, a length of timber placed between wall and fenders will stop them slipping off the face of piles and so needing constant tending.

The appropriate shape for fenders depends on the round of your topsides, height of freeboard, type of caprail and other such characteristics. Some will be found to rest quietly and others to slip about or creep up and over the rail as the boat moves. You will have to experiment to find a type that suits your own boat; also the correct height at which to position them.

Fender cleats

In some conditions fenders take an awful hammering, and the stresses they suffer are transmitted up to their cleats. Unless these are throughbolted, they will surely pull adrift, with consequent damage to hull and loss of fenders. The tiny shiny hooks fitted on a lot of new boats are quite useless. Fenders are best not belayed to guardrails, which, although strong, are too flexible to let the fenders stay in position accurately. Fender lines are best taken round cleats fitted for the purpose and belayed with figures of eight.

The use of head and stern lines, springs and breastropes was described on p 69, and you will need to use them when lying alongside in harbour.

Tender

You will have to decide whether to leave the tender lashed in position or launch it ready for immediate use on making fast. Leave it lashed down if possible, for a towed tender is a considerable nuisance in a confined space. On the other hand you may find it such an obstruction to working around the deck that it would be better out of the way and over the side. If so, think think about lashing it alongside rather than towing it astern.

Routines

An experienced crew will quietly get about the preparation for tying up, but if such a routine is strange to them, they should be carefully briefed in advance. If the task is approached methodically, there should be no problems, but nothing looks and sounds more amateur and unseamanlike than a crew dashing about with ropes and fenders and a skipper bawling at them the while.

Getting a line ashore

Longshoremen and onlookers can usually be persuaded to accept a warp and drop it over a bollard, or at least take a turn around something solid until a crewman can get ashore and make fast properly. It may be necessary to throw a heaving line ashore initially to take out the warp. If no one is about, the boat can be brought alongside and held stationary long enough for a man to *step* ashore either with line in hand or ready to take it at once from hand to hand.

Take no chances at such a time. If you are not absolutely certain of putting a man ashore without risk of injury or immersion, it will be preferable to stand off, get him ashore in the tender and go on from there. A wise skipper will point these things out, firmly, to his crew in advance of arrival. Enthusiasts sometimes need protection from their own willingness.

Having made all possible material preparation, the navigator should ensure that he knows precisely what marks and signals are to be expected as the harbour mouth opens. Also the intended course to be steered once inside, together with the chosen place of berthing, method of making fast and alternative courses of action.

INSIDE THE HAVEN

Once you are in, look around and get yourself orientated as quickly as possible. If you find yourself a little confused and doubtful of the next move—and there will be no shame in that—pause for reflection by slowing down or even anchoring off the fairway. Seek advice if needs be. The harbourmaster is the man you want. He will know all about his harbour—ground, moorings, effect of weather conditions, number of boats present and their movements—and will proffer advice which you are advised to accept as instructions.

Harbourmasters do their level best for all visitors, so reflect that one will have nothing against you personally if he points out a berth that you do not think much of. He will be unlikely to place you where you cannot clear out in emergency, where you will be squeezed flat between a couple of Class I racers, where ships will wash you hourly, or where irate owners will arrive in the early hours and blast you off their mooring. It may be a little distant from the bright lights, fish, chips and beer, ten boats out from the quay, or described as temporary, with a move later.

Take the harbourmaster's goodwill and knowledge for granted and be glad that you are in harbour.

If, exceptionally, there is a choice of berths, use imagination and forethought. You will eventually have to depart and should avoid a berth which might fill up and obstruct easy exit later. When tying up to a trot, match heights of freeboard as closely as possible to avoid damage. Unoccupied mooring buoys will be either private or harbour property. Few owners mind their moorings being used during their absence as a temporary measure; the harbourmaster knows who is away and will often allocate an empty one to you. Otherwise he might be able to let you have a harbour mooring.

Most harbours have regulations stipulating the areas of permitted anchorage exhibited in harbour offices and mentioned in guides. To anchor in a fairway would endanger all users of the waters and, if you are not sure where the proper areas lie, anchor shoreward of any other craft bordering the fairway and enquire of the harbourmaster. The mundane routines of ascertaining depth of water, estimating scope and so on should be automatic, but think about the need for a riding light.

In large harbours many boats lie at anchor and are invisible unless showing a light. In recognised areas of anchorage there may not be a requirement to show a light, and locals, being aware of this, keep clear. You should take care not to blunder into such a region if you are groping about in the dark. When you anchor, unless you are certain that you repose in such an area, exhibit a riding light. It will protect you from collision and also be a great help in finding your boat after a run ashore.

It is foolish to go ashore and leave your boat unattended if there is the slightest chance of her going adrift. Once ashore you will need to keep an eye open for the weather. If holding ground is poor or streams run hard, mooring to two anchors will give peace of mind if you have to leave her for any period of time.

Fees and other matters

I do not want to preach, but I would like to say a word about behaviour in harbours. These are places where, as ashore, folk congregate and have to live in amity with each other. There are accepted conventions and codes of conduct which make life pleasant if followed and uncivilised if ignored.

It is not nice to object to or try to avoid paying harbour dues—the sums involved are small in relation to the facilities provided. If you doubt this, see how you feel on picking up the leading lights and making safely fast in harbour after your first hard time offshore at night. Payment is due, even if you lie to your own anchor, for the use of harbour facilities. Sometimes a mooring is thrown in for good measure—it keeps the place tidy.

Strewn litter is as pollutant afloat as ashore.

Loud radios and other noises late at night are objectionable.

There are many female sailors, some of whom may not care for the use of offshore language in harbour.

Privacy should be respected, so that when necessarily crossing over the decks of other craft, one should go by way of the fore-deck and resist any temptation to peek into hatches and windows.

A ready hand for the other man's boat will sooner or later be repaid in full measure.

Finally, it is gratifying to think that on departure you will be welcome on your next visit. Harbourmasters have long memories.

GOING FOREIGN

Short passages to the coasts of Europe can be made with the use of Admiralty or other British charts. Should you have to make use of foreign ones, remember that soundings will be in metres, not fathoms and feet. We are presently undergoing a complete change of chart notation into the metric system, but there will be a period of some years when charts will be found in various types of measurement. It pays to be sure what sort you are using to navigate.

Buoyage systems will be unfamiliar and should be studied in advance and checked as you sail along. Pay close attention to the cardinal system of marking hazards. Harbour signals can present difficulty and may be totally different from those employed in home waters.

Before leaving the UK, report to Customs, where you will be asked to fill in a form stating details of your journey, boat, crew and so forth. Not only will this save you bother on return but it enables a check to be kept on your movements which is conducive to safety. Leave information about your estimated times of arrival and return with relatives, friends or your Club and notify them of any significant alterations to your itinerary.

On return report directly to Customs for clearance, flying a 'Q' signal flag in your shrouds or carrying the proper light signal at night—a red light close over a white one. Yachts seldom exhibit the lights, and as Customs wharves are usually well lit, the 'Q' flag can be seen and is accepted by night as well as by day. Failure to comply with these requirements is illegal and can land you in trouble. Smuggling should not be attempted, because the penalty can be not only a fine but the impounding of your boat. Besides, Customs people are very decent to yachtsmen and seldom rummage through their boats exhaustively. It would be nice to keep things that way.

Arriving in a foreign harbour, you should fly your ensign and the 'Q' flag or exhibit the lights. Stay aboard until visited by the authorities if you can. In some ports they may not arrive for a considerable time, if at all, and sailors do go ashore beforehand. Neighbouring craft will probably be able to enlighten you about the prevailing customs, but if you are in any doubt, it is sensible to report to the Customs house before leaving the harbour area.

It is universal etiquette for visiting yachts to fly a small 'courtesy' ensign of the country being visited in addition to wearing their own red or blue duster. This is not compulsory, but few yachtsmen omit the gesture of having one visible from their crosstrees when abroad.

Harbour Lore

You will be able to buy stocks of duty-free goods from chandlers around harbours. You will probably not be limited in the amount you buy, but British Customs stipulate the quantities which may be imported on return. If you wish to bring more than the duty-free limit, there is nothing to stop you, but it should be declared on arrival and you should be prepared to pay duty on the excess.

CHAPTER FOUR

The Crew

LEADERSHIP

In the final analysis, the success of any passage rests on the abilities and personality of the man in command. Crews normally take it for granted that their skipper is fully competent to look after their safety and general welfare. Consequently, they will follow his orders and be reluctant to criticise his intentions or actions no matter what doubts they may sometimes entertain.

It is thus up to a skipper to be constantly self-critical and to strive to be worthy of the trust and respect of his crew. It is essential for the family skipper that his wife and children's trust in him is never shattered. This could well result in an abrupt end to family enjoyment afloat.

Leadership can only be based on the principle that you never expect a crew member to do something that you could not do as well yourself, or perhaps a little better. I am not suggesting that septuagenarians shin up masts, but unless you know from personal experience at some time what might be the consequences of asking a crewman to do so, you should not require it of him.

If a difficult or hazardous situation arises afloat, such as may involve taking a calculated risk, much good may come of discussing the position with your crew and hearing their views. However, command cannot be by committee and you will finally have the personal responsibility of taking a decision. Having done so, you must then insist that your orders are obeyed implicitly by all aboard, no matter how pleasantly or unemphatically you care to phrase them. It may be essential at times to subordinate personal relationships to those which should exist between skipper and crew. This might mean, for example, ordering your wife to do something difficult or even hazardous— a thing which you would avoid in circumstances of less stringency.

Orders should be given so clearly, and so unambiguously, as never to need repeating. The greater the need for an order to be correctly executed at the first attempt, the greater the need for deliberate and audible enunciation. Shouting confuses people and rapid speech can be misunderstood.

SLEEP

It is essential that every member of a crew gets enough undisturbed sleep to keep body refreshed and mind clear for watches on deck. Tired men get careless and unobservant, so enough sleep for all is a necessity for safe passage-making. There is often a natural reluctance to retire below and sleep during the day, with a corresponding and overwhelming desire to do so after dark, but a wise skipper will set watches and insist that they are kept. Initially some folk find difficulty in dropping off to sleep in the day but they should be persuaded to lie down on their bunks and relax. Sleep will often ensue. Later on they will crave the opportunity, and sleep will come easily.

The skipper should follow his own precepts and have faith in his alternate watchkeeper. With sufficient crew aboard he may omit himself from regular watches, sleep at convenient times and be on call always. In working out ways of setting up watch-keeping routines to suit your requirements, bear in mind that the traditional four on/four off watch periods interrupted by 2hr dogwatches are not really suitable to a small crew.

The basic requirement on a small boat is that the watch on deck should be restricted to the minimum number of men needed for efficiency in prevailing circumstances. These can be widely variable, but it is always wise to have reserves off watch who can be roused in exigencies. Let us consider the case of a small boat on a week's passage with a crew of three aboard. At least a couple of nights are going to be spent offshore.

By day, in reasonable conditions, one man can be expected to trim sail, helm and keep notes for the log—alterations to course, weather changes and so on from which navigation can continue; 2hr of such activity would not be an onerous watch and, if he were keen and alert, could be extended to 3 or even 4hr. All aboard could then count on at least 4hr unbroken sleep and maybe more.

At night, with increased eyestrain and the need for extra vigilance, a turn on the helm should seldom exceed 2hr even in good weather. As summer nights are short, three such watches will cover the period of total darkness, after which longer tricks can be taken.

In more adverse conditions it is likely that two men per watch will be needed. The crew can then be rotated like this. One man does a sensible spell on the helm—say 2hr—with the other chap dressed in oilskins and safety harness below, where he can doze but be ready to get on deck if called. On change of watch the standby brews up, calls the sleeper and takes the helm. The sleeper then comes to standby and the helmsman undresses and turns in. In this way each man gets 2hr sleep and the chance of following it with a snooze below if he is lucky.

Experiments will help you to arrive at sensible solutions to your own problems, and there are manifold variations on the watch-keeping theme. It is a good thing never to allow crew to remain on deck unnecessarily if you consider that this might give rise to problems later on. Without being accused of hogging it, a sensible skipper keeps himself topped up with sleep against a time when he might perforce have a long and arduous period on deck.

FOOD AND WARMTH

Warmth comes from internal fuel and external protection. No matter how good your insulation against the elements, a lack of food will eventually bring on the feelings and effects of cold. Every cruising boat needs a means of cooking under way and this means at least one ring, either gimballed or fiddled to prevent spillage. Plenty of hot drinks keep a crew happy, but have to be supplemented with quantities of solid food from time to time.

It does not matter whether food is hot or cold, for human bodies convert all to energy, but hot food does much for morale. Tinned soups are useful items to stow aboard, and if a couple of eggs are whipped up in them as they are heating, the mixture is palatable and sustaining. Slices of soft cheese melting cosily into piping hot soup are succulent and nourishing, but such farradiddles only fill in the gaps. At least one good hot meal per day is needed.

In bad weather an attempt should be made to prepare something hot in a thermos for the man at the helm and other crew on deck to take at intervals, together with sandwiches. If a meal can be got together, it can be eaten from a basin with the aid of a spoon when the motion precludes the use of plates, knives, forks and other sophisticated tools. If conditions get really bad and you see that your crew needs relief and a hot meal, it is wise to heave-to for long enough for them to get something to eat and perhaps get forty winks.

Take care with alcohol. It confers a spurious warmth, but is in fact a depressant, and its user will feel colder than before when its effects wear off. If a man can be reasonably sure of a couple of hours sleep, however, a tot will help him drop off.

Once a man gets wet, he will sooner or later feel cold, and nothing will really serve to warm him again except a change of clothing from the skin out. The first essential is to see that your oilies are leakproof. One-piece suits afford excellent protection, but are awkward to use unless very well designed. They can seldom be donned in a hurry. Unless the trousers of two-piece suits come really high up on the chest they will admit water underneath the jacket and on to the small of the back. Some folk wear knee-length coats of the fisherman type, but these are cumbersome if you have to kneel or crawl about the deck. The short manchester boots are more fashionable than wellingtons but less effective, and the bottoms of trouserlegs tend to ride up over them and let in water. Elastic loops sewn on to the hems and passed under the insteps of the boots may help, but the best solution is to have calf-length boots and lash the bottom of the trousers around the ankles. Wetsuits are smelly, unhygienic and unsuitable for cruising purposes.

Plenty of loose thick clothing is needed to keep out the chill at sea. Knitted garments let the wind through unless there is a shirt, or vest and shirt, beneath them. Serge trousers are far warmer than jeans and ex-naval ones can be bought cheap from surplus stores. Even in high summer, nights are chilly and a man going on watch should think about getting into thick togs and oilies. The main thing is to keep out draughts, which cause the body to cool through the evaporation of sweat. Everyone aboard should have at least one complete change of clothing stowed in a waterproof bag; two changes are better still if stowage permits.

Once a garment has got soaked with salt water, it will be hygroscopic and remain damp as long as there is any humidity in the atmosphere, as is normal in a marine environment. Only by washing the salt out can they be successfully dried. It is therefore necessary to prevent water getting down below. A lot is taken there by wet oilies, so a routine is necessary to ensure that they are taken off at the bottom of the companionway and then stowed as far aft as possible. This could be under the cockpit, in an empty quarterberth or in lockers allotted for the purpose.

Bedding should obviously stay as dry as possible. Blankets are a curse. Not only do they seem to sop up moisture but they flop around and deposit fluff everywhere. A good terylene sleeping bag is infinitely preferable as long as the zip is stout and rustproof. They roll up small and can be conveniently stowed in large polythene bags. Pyjamas are also likely to get wet, and the practice of sleeping raw in a good sleeping bag is about the best way to keep warm and dry. If an inner liner is used, it will do away with the need for laundering the bag at frequent intervals.

BODILY FITNESS

Constipation is the curse of the cruising classes, but is not something that needs to be worried about. I understand the record is 103 days! If the condition bothers you, it can be combated with plenty of roughage in your diet—All-Bran and that sort of thing. Fruit, fruitjuice and green vegetables are also good in this respect, but peas, beans and other pulses create wind, which can cause stomach cramps and unpopularity. Most of us go for food in tins, which is tasty and simple to prepare, but such concentrated stuff is binding. The lavish use of laxatives should be guarded against; their results are unpredictable and often drastic.

Seasickness is a mysterious complaint and there are those who contend that constipation is a contributory factor, so if it can be avoided so much the better.

You don't have to be a Hercules to go cruising. Many of us are sedentary workers, but a regime of bodybuilding is uncalled for. What is important is that you should think hard before going on passage if you are a bit under the weather. If you have a temperature, heavy cold, pulled muscle or other condition which might deteriorate, you could end up as a liability to the rest of the crew. It might be more sensible to stay ashore and swallow your disappointment.

Even more important is to avoid taking on a passage which could overtax your strength or stamina. Some boats are heavy to work, and it is an easy thing for a soft or elderly person to slip a disc or suffer a rupture. Both complaints, which are not the only ones to fear, are disabling and can be extremely painful. If you are a family skipper, you will know the limitations of your boat, but beware of possible conditions that could render you inoperative. Very often you will be the sole effective crew, and inability to cope could endanger your family.

PERSONALITY PROBLEMS

Short of marriage or a prison cell, life aboard a small boat is as intimately close as people are likely to live together. Under the irks and stresses of passage-making temperaments may come to the fore, and a skipper has to be alive to problems brewing amongst members of his crew. He has to be much of a psychologist and mediator in solving them. Tolerance and patience on all sides are called for and will help smooth out many difficult situations.

Much irritation stems from silly little things like tooth-picking, whistling under the breath and odd table manners. It is often extremely difficult to broach such matters and the personality of the offender will determine whether you should have a quiet aside with him, make a jocular reference or in some other way bring the matter into the open for discussion.

Untidiness is most annoying and should be tackled before it gets contagious. Failure to restow gear in its place could hazard the boat. Strewing personal belongings all over the ship is commonplace. The best way to combat it is to see that each crew member has an allotted space in which his gear is inviolable. Anything then found lying about is fair game to be dropped into a wet and smelly bilge.

A few people are congenitally lazy and will go to great lengths to bestow their duties on willing and unsuspecting horses. You should quietly insist that a man fully and correctly does everything that is asked of him or, sooner or later, he will become guilty of a bad sin of omission. I once went dangerously adrift and lost a perfectly good anchor because the man who shackled it into the cable had been too tired to search for the shackle key which he had himself previously mislaid.

Personal uncleanliness is mercifully rare but not unknown. It is not a matter that can be resolved satisfactorily. The only remedy is to discharge the offender as soon as possible.

Inexperienced crew men are usually a pleasure to have aboard. They are eager to muck in, learn and generally improve their abilities, but the half-experienced know-all is a terrible menace. Although a really experienced man may well know far more than his skipper, he is unlikely to do more than carry his fair load; he will offer useful advice if asked but otherwise probably keep silent. The blowhard, on the other hand, will for ever vociferously put forward his opnions, undermine the skipper's authority by arguing about his decisions and generally make a confounded nuisance of himself. He should never be trusted to take charge of a watch, and this he will always try to do.

A good skipper leads his crew and refrains from bullying them. He should be able to do everything about the ship a little better than they can without making them feel conscious of their own inexperience or shortcomings. If he can do all this and maintain an air of assurance when his own confidence is slightly shaky, things will go well in spite of minor frictions and upsets.

CHAPTER FIVE

The Boat

COSTS

The purchase price of a boat may be well short of its final cost in full sailing trim, and will have to be judged against what it includes. Many essential items can be overlooked in the first flush of inexperienced enthusiasm, and later the knowledge will come that other things, in no way luxuries, should be bought for enjoyment of one's sailing in full measure. Initial purchase price could be as little as two-thirds of the eventual expenditure. Ancillary items can amount to an astonishing sum, but a scantily equipped boat can be a source of nagging dissatisfaction. Certain gear, such as a minimum quantity of safety gear, must not be omitted. More than that, however, as experience grows, an owner starts to realise how much is really desirable in the interests of ease of handling, comfort and other personal requirements.

Many owners find that they would like to trail their boats, and there is a limit to the size and weight of a cruiser which can be moved in this fashion. The cost of a trailer then arises, and they are not cheap. There is also the problem of the ability of the family car to deal with the load. Even if it is powerful enough, it may have to be fitted with a towbar.

Trailing apart, there is almost inevitably the need to have some sort of laying-up cradle or trolley. These adjuncts must be stoutly constructed of good materials, and so are not inexpensive. The laying-up covers have to be bought or made. You can learn to cut, fit and sew them, of course, and are advised to get a copy of the *Admiralty Sailmakers' Handbook*, which will set out in simple terms the way to approach all tasks of this sort. Polythene is cheap and can serve at a pinch for winter covers, but even the heaviest grades are relatively fragile enough to need frequent replacement and are greatly subject to weather damage. If a boat is to be left unattended for long periods, it is better to use covers of stouter material such as canvas or a synthetic fabric.

Other covers may be needed, eg to lash over a non-draining cockpit both ashore and afloat, as is customary with powerboats. Their method of attachment must be considered. Small cleats, buttons, hooks and eyes and so on are much more convenient than yards of lashings, but 5p here and 10p there all add up. Sailcovers are essential to protect sails left on booms from dirt and deterioration (to unbend and stow main and mizzen each time you tie up is a dreadful and needless chore). Spray hood and dodgers are a great comfort to the crew in cold wet conditions. Even if you make them, the material will cost quite a bit. Then you may need a ladder or staging for fitting out and maintenance.

Once bought, these and similar capital items should last a long time, but they do not end the list. Some recurrent expenditure usually is inescapable—insurance, replacement of gear, maintenance materials like paint, antifouling, resin, glassfibre, timber, tools, brushes, thinners, cleaning materials. Then there is the question of moorings. One may have to pay rent or even buy a mooring and pay rent for the space. There is the possible cost of a haulout, scrub and relaunch, for which you may have to hire a crane. The list is lengthy. There are well hidden items such as the cost of extra car mileage if your boat winters a long way from home.

You can take a sanguine view and argue that annual recurrent expenditure should be met out of 'current' cash, but it is well to confirm that this will be available when needed. If, for instance, you buy your boat on mortgage, it will clearly reduce the amount of 'current' cash to such an extent as might make annual expenditure hard to find. Desiderata increase considerably with size of boat, and this fact should be kept in mind, together with the general considerations, when you are thinking of making an initial purchase.

Certain advantages attach to British Registration of a boat. Without registration you cannot raise a mortgage, the cheapest way of buying a boat on extended terms, as the interest charges are subject to tax relief. The current cost of registration is just under £40 and a résumé is set out in *Reed's Almanac*. This leads on to the point that a cruising boat needs such an almanac annually, and one has to have charts, tidal atlases, navigation equipment and so on. These have previously been mentioned, but readers are advised to study this book thoroughly with an eye to the costs implied in each chapter.

There is almost always an irresistible urge to stretch beyond one's practical means, and this should be resisted. Enjoyment does not by any means reside in the possession of the biggest or shiniest boat afloat. Insufficient allowance for the cost of ancillaries and recurrent expenditure has ruined the pleasure of many a man and turned his gaze away from the sea.

CHOOSING A BOAT

No one should be beguiled into acquiring a boat which is not, or cannot be rendered, suitable for his particular needs. Crewing in different boats is the best way of defining your requirements before purchase, as is participation in their maintenance and fitting-out.

Size

'Popular' boats, which concern readers, range from about 16ft to 30ft length overall (LOA). Broadly speaking, boats under some 22ft LOA are unfit to take offshore and should be confined to sheltered waters. Speed is principally a function of waterline length (LWL) and very small boats are too slow for serious passage-making. They are badly affected by sea conditions, which cause discomfort and inability to work effectively around the deck, and they need frequent and early reduction of sail as the breeze strengthens.

Above 25ft LOA the handling of sails and ground tackle becomes onerous for a family man, who is often obliged to tend his boat with little, if any, assistance from his crew. One should therefore be careful not to choose a boat which is too small for its task nor one which, even if fitted with plenty of mechanical aids, is too large for its minimum crew to handle effectively.

Individual sail areas can be cut down by choosing a ketch or yawl rig and cutter headsails; the latter can be automatically furled with great ease and convenience. Probably, however, the greatest limitation on acceptable size lies in the weight of hull and ground tackle. Mechanical aids are considered later, but the backbreaking implications of mooring, warping and anchor work must be given thought.

Headroom

Standing headroom, desirable but not essential, is unlikely to be found in boats much under 27ft LOA and even these may have unduly high freeboards and prominent coachroofs. Such things cause extra windage and can look very ugly. In the extreme they can make a boat hard to handle in stiff conditions, and it is better to settle for *really good* sitting headroom and an attractive sea-worthy vessel. Such headroom needs to be carefully designed to avoid neck and shoulders coming into contact with sidedecks and interior protrusions.

Capacity

To pack too many crew into a boat creates an unacceptable standard of discomfort. Room is needed for gear and belongings, navigation, cooking, eating, washing and a loo of some sort. To try to add four berths to this in a 20ft hull is not realistic. Beware of smooth-talking salesmen—only experience afloat is likely to highlight the snags.

Shape

Underwater configuration is varied and important. Long keels can bestow less draught, some self-sailing ability, ease of drying out and more headroom because the cabin sole is set lower into the hull than with canoe-type bilges. If long keels are very shallow, they are often supplemented by bilge keels, which are said to confer stability in the rolling plane, or a centreboard, which assists windward performances by increasing the effective draught. For cruising purposes there is a lot to be said in favour of a long keel. A deep narrow fin keel causes extreme sensitivity to helm and difficulties in drying out, although providing optimum windward performance and speed. Twin ballast keels are detrimental to windward work, but tend to damp rolling and make beaching or drying out an easy matter. Multihulls are fast, dry and heel little, as well as offering much accommodation for their LOA. Unless their sail area is carefully matched to the wind strength they can be capsized and are not intrinsically self-righting, which leaves them open to doubt for serious cruising. There is, however, continuous research and development in the multihull field and they should not be disregarded lightly in view of their manifold advantages.

Construction

Steel and ferrocement are heavy materials and not used for the small classes. Aluminium is very suitable but expensive, difficult to work and infrequently found.

Today's material is glass reinforced plastic (GRP, glassfibre, fibreglass, resinglass—all mean the same thing). Its quality is virtually impossible to determine after moulding and depends on the integrity of the workmanship. Badly moulded GRP can be structurally weak, but reputable moulders mostly produce under Lloyd's supervision. They can supply you with a series production certificate or, for a little extra, an individual certificate of moulding. Their products are not cheap, but provide advantages for the purposes of insurance, safety, resale and minimisation of depreciation. The maintenance of a GRP boat is reduced to a low level compared with other materials, and it is well within the capability of the average owner to modify and repair his own craft.

Wood is the traditional boat-building material, and there are many sorts of timber and many ways of using them. New boats are seldom built of wood, and a survey of any secondhand boat will disclose the state of the timber used in its construction.

Clinkerbuilt craft are light and tend to flex quite a bit when driven hard. They become leaky with age, a condition almost impossible to remedy. Clinker is tedious to repair in the event of damage. For all these reasons a clinkerbuilt boat may not be considered entirely suitable for prolonged and serious cruising. It is not advisable to buy a secondhand boat of this type which has been hauled out ashore for any length of time. You may be told that it will take up after it has been afloat for a few days, but this statement should not be taken at face value.

Carvel hulls look and feel good. They are relatively easy to repair, but periodic attention must be given to their caulking. Strip planking is a variety of carvel building in which caulking is omitted and the planks are glued and fastened edge to edge. Repair is difficult and, as this method is favoured among amateur builders, gluing may be suspect and give rise to future trouble. The absence of caulking allows the wood no room for movement, and strip-planked hulls often appear wavy. This in no way affects their integrity, but if looks offend, the only remedy is to plane or sand down and this weakens the planking.

Hot or cold moulded plywood or veneers produce a mono-lithic hull which is leak-free and very strong for its weight. Such a hull will be longlasting and highly resistant to marine attack, but is not simple to repair.

Sheets of ply mean hard chines and strength for weight. Gluing, again, can be suspect, but repair is fairly easy. Sheet ply is very often used to build leak-free decks and superstructures, and takes well to sheathing with GRP for added strength and integrity.

Such sheathing is often used to protect underwater timber from marine attack but needs to be carefully applied to bare wood. It often fails to adhere to old, previously painted or varnished surfaces, no matter how carefully they are rubbed down. There are other patent methods of sheathing timber, such as Cascover, which are expensive but afford good protection if properly done.

Wooden boats have their keels attached by metal bolts which deteriorate with time, and consequently are a potential source of danger. Inspection is a matter of some difficulty and expensive if carried out professionally, but is not really a job for an amateur. Any survey of an old boat should include inspection of keelbolts.

Displacement

A tendency to heavy displacement is usually thought to be a desirable feature of any cruising boat, and the weight of boats of a similar LOA can be highly variable. Lightweight boats, with less weight of material and smaller sails and rigging, should not only cost less but call for less manual effort in handling and maintenance. On the other hand they can be too lively in their motion, wet and uncomfortable in a seaway, heel too readily or excessively and be hard to keep driving through bad conditions. Heavier displacement confers stability and habitability in bad weather, and these are factors conducive to safe and efficient sailing. There is, however, no intrinsic unseaworthiness in a well found light-displacement boat, and it will be faster and more responsive in light airs. For those of us who choose our weather and indulge in restricted passage-making, it will probably be more economical of cash and effort to settle for a light-displacement boat and chance the occasional discomforts of a blow.

Whatever boat you finally choose, make sure that it is *good of its type*. There is a vast difference between makes. Draw a contrast between a pretty, weatherly boat with a low profile and one of the same dimensions which is topheavy, scantily fitted with undersized rigging, light in scantlings, and of uncertain construction. A bad boat will not even cost less, but this is utterly beside the point.

Even among well found and apparently suitable boats there are differences of behaviour afloat, and it is not wise to buy without having a trial sail. The heavier the weather the better, within reason of course, as a craft which sails and handles well in light airs may show a different face in a press of wind and lop of sea. Excessive, even unacceptable, weatherhelm may develop. This can be a basic design fault and uncorrectable by any trimming or tuning. There may be excessive heel which, although quite safe, is intolerably uncomfortable; many wives find heeling a bit frightening and could be put off sailing completely if you buy the wrong boat. Heeling is normally quite uncorrectable except by adding inside ballast; this will alter the designed characteristics of a hull and is not a recommended practice.

Water gets everywhere at sea, and such little things as missing or badly designed scuppers and drainage apertures may make life unhappy. Water leaks through the most unexpected places, with consequent discomfort, and it is often frustrating to have to trace and plug a small persistent leak. This sort of thing, and many other stupid little matters which you cannot know about unless you have had some sea experience beforehand, are important for you to discover before investing a large sum of cash in something you hope will be pleasurable.

Think very hard if you are tempted to buy something for conversion. Boats are designed and built for a specific purpose and one which has been transmogrified for a different role is unlikely to be satisfactory. One brings to mind the ship's lifeboat, often to be had for a very small sum. No matter how sound and well maintained, it is a pulling boat, and no keel and sails will ever transform it into an effective sailing boat. The addition of tophamper might even render it unseaworthy. Such unhappy hybrids can often be seen advertised as 'roomy family LBC cruiser . . .'

On the other hand certain boats do lend themselves to most successful conversion to cruisers. The ex-metre boats are basically weatherly and fast, though a little narrow-gutted when converted, and the working boat of the trawler or ferry punt type can be turned into a roomy and eminently seakindly cruising boat.

Regrettably most hulls of this sort are elderly, and a survey will show up the effects of age and weaknesses brought about by change of purpose or indifferent workmanship. Conversion is often amateur in concept and execution, and done in the lack of fundamental knowledge and ability. It is finicky and time-consuming work, best not attempted by one who may spend much time and money and end up with an unsaleable 'clum-bungay'.

RIGGING, FITTINGS, SAILS AND SPARS

Most popular boats are sold fitted out to a standard specification. This varies widely between models, and it is worth finding out exactly what you are getting for your money. Obliging boatyards *might* be prepared to offer you a choice of fittings and so on, but special requirements will be expensive if they stray outside the limits of boatyard stocks. If you complete a boat from kit or hull, which provides a way of saving considerable amounts of money in return for your labour, the choice of fittings can be to suit your own pocket and requirements. As prices vary widely from place to place and shop to shop, you can save money by looking around. Marine auctions are good places to find a bargain if you choose carefully and do not let discretion be overcome by enthusiasm.

The first thing to do, if fittings are to be chosen, is to decide whether you can conscientiously keep your boat up to full 'yacht' standard, with varnished brightwork, gleaming metal and unsullied paint, or are content to settle for a working cruiser, with little varnish, dull metal and much paint, presenting a neat but not gaudy appearance. A scruffy 'yacht' looks terrible and proper maintenance can take up more time than a busy man can spare, whereas a less pretentious cruiser can be kept clean and neat with considerably less effort. This permits more time for sailing and so may be preferable.

Rigging and fittings
The choice lies between stainless or galvanised wire and end fittings, together with other items like chainplates, bottlescrews, cleats, fairleads, pulpit, guardrails and the host of other essentials around the deck.

Size for size stainless steel fittings are somewhat stronger, but unless welded joints are impeccable, they can break abruptly, whereas galvanised fittings show signs of stretch or distortion beforehand. Stainless steel is much more expensive, but this is defended on the grounds that it lasts longer. This is not necessarily true in the case of cruising boats, since stresses are generally lower than on boats which are regularly raced, but galvanised wire and fittings need regular inspection and attention if they are to give lasting service. This means essentially that damage to galvanised surfaces must be protected with paint or rust preventive, and that rigging wire needs an annual soaking in a mixture of petrol and linseed oil. The petrol evaporates and leaves a coating of oxydised oil over the zinc. This also penetrates the wire into the fibre core and effectively lubricates it. I know of many fine cruisers fitted throughout with galvanised wire which has lasted 6–7 years without giving trouble.

Whatever the choice of metal, it is essential to ensure that rigging and fittings are man enough for their job. They are often kept to a dubious minimum size where boats are built down to a price, and undersized gear is never acceptable. Not only is the safety factor greatly reduced, but rigging which is constantly stressed to near its safe working limits will have a comparatively short life. It is only fractionally more costly to fit a sensible size all round and it will certainly pay off in the long run on grounds of both safety and economy.

Mechanical aids

Without getting gadgety, the more mechanical aids an owner can afford to fit the less will be the physical effort needed aboard. In the case of shorthanded boats like family cruisers, this can mean the difference between happy and successful passage-making and very limited activities.

Sailhandling

Just hoisting a sail is not particularly heavy work, but it is often difficult to get a taut luff on main and foresails after reefing or during a blow. If you can afford halyard winches, they will ease the task enormously; with big sails a geared winch is a real boon. Self-stowing winches used with wire halyards are, in addition, extremely neat and tidy. Such gear can be used with ease and safety to hoist a man in a bosun's chair if it is necessary to go aloft for any reason.

Sheet winches are really essential on craft of any size to handle foresails efficiently and, again, two-speed models permit accurate trimming without great physical effort. In most cases mainsheets can be handled by using a suitable purchase, but on larger boats (say, over 26ft LOA) it is convenient to have this backed up by a winch.

Winches tend to be inordinately expensive if they are at all sophisticated, but simple stout galvanised models are to be had and are quite efficient for cruising purposes.

Ground tackle

An anchor winch is a very desirable item indeed, for the most backbreaking and frustrating job aboard is getting in the anchor. Winches range from simple galvanised hand-operated ones to electric or hydraulic patterns driven from an engine or heavy batteries. They can also be used for kedging off or getting heavy moorings inboard.

Lifting inboard
Heavy weights often have to be got aboard—tenders, provisions, fuel and water containers, etc—and hauling such items over the rail can be hard and awkward work. A form of multiple hoist, such as the Haltrac midget, is easy to stow and weighs surprisingly little. If attached to the end of a boom, which can be swung in and out over the side with no difficulty, it serves as a poor man's derrick and will have many uses. Such a device is capable of lifting an unconscious man out of the water in the case of an accident.

Self-steering gear
This useful adjunct to shorthanded sailing is to be had in many types, but most gear is expensive and you must seriously think if you really need one. Many boats will sail themselves quite happily for long periods if sail and helm are trimmed in balance. A boat's ability to do this is one of the things to bear in mind when sailing a trial with a view to purchase. Any boat which is over-sensitive on the helm, as are most finkeelers with a separate rudder, is not likely to have much self-sailing propensity. If you buy one of these and wish to be relieved of the tedium of helming every second of your watch, you may have to buy a self-steering gear.

Sails
Synthetic cloth is the automatic choice for sails, except perhaps in the tropics, where it will be affected by perpetual strong sunlight. Your decision will be as to the number of sails you need to cruise successfully, and outfits included in the purchase price of a boat vary widely. Some boats, usually racing craft, are sold without sails, some with just a main and one foresail and some with a complete suit, although this is not common. Sails are expensive, but as they are your means of power, they must be

satisfactory in performance. It is surprising how the price for seemingly identical sails can vary between makers. It certainly pays to obtain quotations as widely as possible before buying. A cheaper estimate than you allowed for, from a maker of repute, of course, will mean that you can order in a heavier cloth which will give longer service (so long as you do not order something very stiff).

It is possible to get afloat with just a mainsail and a general purpose jib, but time will prove the need for a small jib for heavy weather and a large one to let you make the most of light airs. In the interests of safety, buy them in that order. Unless you intend to race, a spinnaker and its associated gear are not needed and the money can be spent more wisely in getting together a greater variety of headsails and, probably, a spare main.

Unless you are in the habit of bagging and stowing your mainsail, which is a nuisance when cruising, a sailcover is necessary to protect it from dirt and the deleterious effects of sunlight. The same applies to mizzens, of course.

SAFETY EQUIPMENT

To go sailing in safety both boat and crew need certain basic safety equipment, and there is other optional gear which is an added safeguard against misfortune if it can be afforded. The basic equipment is detailed in Chapter 6 and only really mentioned here in connection with costs. You cannot afford to skimp in this field if you are prudent.

Additionally no one should sail any distance without the means of navigating, and the gear needed for this purpose has already been detailed.

Additional useful equipment could be a radio transmitter/receiver, Aldis lamp with batteries and spare bulb, signal flags 'V' (I need assistance) and 'W' (I need medical assistance). A full set of flags is quite superfluous for coastal passage-making.

DOMESTIC EQUIPMENT

You will wish to cruise in comparative comfort as well as in safety. The following items are virtually indispensable in the long term and you can accumulate them over a period of time if needs be, though many men camp out in a bare boat during the first season:

1. Cooking stove. This can vary from a single ring to a large stove with grill and oven.
2. Pots, pans, cutlery and crockery.
3. Sink.
4. Supply of fresh water, ranging from a jerrycan to moulded-in tanks with pump or pressure supply.
5. Food containers.
6. Cleaning gear and material.
7. A toilet—bucket and chuck-it, pump model, or chemical with or without venting over the side. The choice is wide.
8. Lighting—electric from battery or main circuit, neon, paraffin, or gas.
9. Bunk cushions—costly items, although they can be homemade.
10. Canvas leeboards for bunks, essential for sleeping under way.

There is probably a lot more but this will do to go on with. You will also have to think about locker space. Some craft are designed and fitted with plenty of large and small lockers and drawers, but others simply have empty areas below berths, cockpit seats and so on. Adequate lockers have a great bearing on habitability.

ENGINES

A motor of some description is essential nowadays, if only for getting in and out of harbours. As an alternative means of propulsion it is a safety factor, and it is also a means of keeping to a cruising schedule or getting back to base on time. The choice is whether to have inboard or outboard and of what type, size and make. This may be purely a question of cost.

Outboards

A reliable outboard, of which there are many, is much cheaper to buy than an inboard, and is versatile, as it can also be used on the tender. For work around harbour and elsewhere in reasonably calm conditions a good outboard will serve to propel a boat of up to about 25ft, but its use will have inherent disadvantages.

Outboards have to be lifted in and out of the boat and on and off a bracket of some sort. However, there are patent spring-loaded brackets which make immersion and extraction painless. Outboards are not much use in a seaway, as the propeller comes out of the water when the stern lifts and they can be swamped by a wave. They can be noisy and vibrate excessively. They are extravagant with fuel and subject to plug trouble. On the credit side they are easy to service and maintain. However, for serious cruising it is really necessary to have an inboard engine.

Inboards

If you buy a boat complete with engine in the purchase price, you may only have to decide among a choice of alternative models. Again it will be a matter of price. If you buy a boat without an inboard and intend to fit one later, take care that the hull is suitable to accept it and that you will be able to fit it—complete with bearers, sterntube, shafting, exhaust, waterpipes and so on. Very often craft are so designed that the motor has to be installed before the superstructure is bonded on, so be careful that you do not find yourself having almost to tear open and rebuild your boat. Look at the engine in the model of your choice and make sure that it can be removed for overhaul or replacement later.

The accessibility of glands, oildrains, plugs, magnetos and other parts of the system must be considered critically. You must be able to get at all vital points without undue difficulty, remembering that an engine usually will give trouble when times are hard and it is important to be able to rectify it quickly and easily.

Fuel tanks will be needed and some craft have them moulded

in or carefully fitted together with the pipes, Again, if you intend to fit an engine later, consider the problem of tankage and piping. Similar thought will have to be given to the mounting and removal of accumulators, with attendant wiring circuits, and to the positioning, mounting and connection of engine controls.

Petrol or diesel
In the present state of the technology, petrol engines are lighter and less expensive than diesels for the same power. In the smaller sizes they are smoother running and much quieter. They are harder to maintain in good working order, since their electrical systems are vulnerable to damp, although trouble can be minimised by careful fitting and maintenance. They use more per mile of a more expensive fuel, but this argument can be overdone. The mileage run per season by the average sailing cruiser's auxiliary is small and a balance has to be struck between initial costs and running costs. It would take many years for the difference between, say, £250 for a small petrol engine and £350 for an equivalent diesel model to be recouped by the differential in running costs.

The choice is more critical for powerboat owners, who may well be able to make up the difference in a comparatively short time. Other factors like bulk, weight, responsiveness and reliability have to be weighed against the requirements of a particular hull.

On grounds of reliability the odds are heavily in favour of a diesel engine—properly maintained, of course. Once the first 'chonk' is heard, the motor will run unhesitatingly until the fuel is exhausted. It is a very heartening sound in times of trouble. A diesel will very seldom give any bother as long as the fuel is carefully filtered and fuel piping so installed that airlocks cannot develop under any sea conditions.

Maintenance
Auxiliary motors are often neglected until they rebel, and it is sensible to stick to a regular maintenance schedule. Strangely

enough they deteriorate more quickly when they are not regularly used. Damp settles on them and is not dispersed by the heat of running. Sump oil and lubricant in cylinders settle and the engine starts up and runs a little dry after a lengthy period of inaction. Accumulators lose their charge and small areas of corrosion in the wiring circuits go unnoticed. Sediment will settle at the bottom of tanks and piping and be taken into carburettors and cylinders on starting up.

So, even if not used for propulsion, inboards should be run at regular intervals, be kept clean and free from damp, have their oil changed regularly and all other action taken in accordance with the maker's handbook. It is very important to 'winterise' them properly in accordance with instructions, particular care being taken to drain out all cooling water to avoid freezing and consequent major damage.

TENDERS

Correct selection of a tender can make all the difference between carefree cruising and a constant nagging worry. It should be accepted that it is not really feasible to tow a tender when on passage; it must somehow be stowed on board. In small cruisers the problem is how to do this. No dinghy under 7ft can be considered stable or capacious enough to serve the general purposes of a cruising tender. Taking this size as a minimum it will be seen that there is seldom room on the coachroof or foredeck of a small cruiser to accommodate one. In craft of, say, 27ft and over there may be room to stow a tailormade hard dinghy on the coachroof, but for most of us the only answer is an inflatable.

By partial deflation it is possible to stow quite capacious dinghies on deck. Most models have at least two airchambers, which lie either fore and aft or one on either side. The former type can be satisfactorily stowed by completely deflating one half and folding it back upon the other. This reduces the length to something like 4ft, allowing it to be stowed on most coachroofs. The side by side type will have to be partially deflated all round and squeezed together to lie in such a space. This is not so convenient, for if the dinghy has to be used in emergency and launched as it stands, it will need two pumping operations to inflate it fully. Large valves passing great quantities of air from a man-size pump are to be preferred to smaller ones, as the tender can be inflated more easily and rapidly.

The tender should be lashed securely in place with strops having some means of quick release. Using line for this purpose has disadvantages; if it has to be severed quickly, the presence of a knife around an inflatable is undesirable. The best thing is nylon webbing with quick release buckles as are fitted to personal harness.

During the night the normal drop in temperature will cause the inflated half of a tender to become soft, so that it is loose in its lashings. Do not fiddle about readjusting them, but simply pump in more air to inflate the airchamber. To this end the air valve should be easily accessible.

Few tenders are equipped with an anchor, but it makes sense to have a small folding grapnel and 50ft of line permanently aboard. A lost oar and swiftly running stream can put a tender well offshore in a short time.

A long stout painter is desirable, as tenders are often tied up alongshore for long periods in regions of great rise and fall. It is inconvenient to find your transport either 20ft under water or hanging high and dry halfway down the harbour wall.

Maintenance

Tenders are often neglected beasts, which is a pity because they are both useful and costly to replace. A wooden boat needs scraping, patching, varnishing and painting like any other boat. Inflatables are affected by salt, oil, sand, grit and other foreign matter, including seagull excrement, which is corrosive and highly adhesive. They should be hosed down with fresh water each time they are stowed away, making sure that all foreign matter is washed out of crevices. During the winter inflatables are best inflated and hung up somewhere after cleaning. If hanging space is not available, they should be cleaned, dried, thoroughly covered with talc and then lightly rolled up and stored in a dry place.

Identification

A tender should be marked with the name of its parent boat and, if you wish, its own whimsical name. This seems to be one area where imagination is given rein by otherwise serious minded owners, the names of whose boats themselves are often exotic. For example, I once met a lovely little clinker dinghy adorning the hard at Salcombe and showing this legend on its little transom: 'Oui-oui. Tender to Piscary'.

Practically speaking, an insurance claim for a lost dinghy is unlikely to succeed if the identifying marking is absent. Also, a dinghy adrift is more often than not returned to its owner by the finder as long as he can trace him. The finding of an abandoned dinghy is a matter to be reported to police or the Receiver of Wrecks in the locality. Obviously there is a possibility that its occupants might have been in trouble at sea.

LAYING UP

Each winter your boat will have to be laid up and fitted out for the following season. It can remain afloat in quiet waters or in a mudberth, when the interior work can be done, followed by a haul-out for painting and antifouling near launching time. Most owners prefer, if at all possible, to lay up ashore and this costs money—some initial and some recurrent.

A towable trailer which can be immersed and used to launch and bring your boat ashore will also permit it to be taken 'home to roost' in a garage, barn or under some form of temporary cover. Many small cruisers and powerboats are dealt with in this way, and the cost of the trailer has to be added to the purchase price. This is offset by the fact that you will not have to pay fees for hauling out and a winter's hard standing. It is possible to build a trailer based on a caravan or lorry chassis, or from proprietary parts. If you use a trailer on the roads, make yourself familiar with Road Traffic Act restrictions on size of tow, lighting and braking regulations and so on.

If towing is not used, a boat can still be got ashore on a mobile cradle made up in similar fashion to a trailer but much cruder in design and construction. Such an item can even be built of timber providing it is stout enough for the purpose. If you are lucky enough to have the use of a hard slipway and standing, it may not even be necessary to have wheels on the cradle. It can be levered and hauled about on rollers, such as lengths of scaffolding. Plenty of grease on rollers and planks used helps enormously in the operation, which is known as 'striking over' and is common in boatyards.

You can, alternatively, lift out your boat by crane and set it into a static cradle, which can be bolted up in situ and dismantled for storing away in the summer. The crane can, at the same time, be used to unstep any mast that goes through to the keel. If employing a crane, make sure of your insurance position.

VALUATION, DEPRECIATION AND INSURANCE

Valuation
People change their boats pretty frequently, it seems, and although you may not have the slightest intention of ever selling your darling, your abilities will improve and your requirements probably alter as a consequence of that improvement. It is as well to cast an eye to the future when you are buying.

Firstly, fashions in boats change as in everything else, and novel boats of possibly extreme type appeal to a restricted number of sailors and only for a limited length of time. These are principally in the racing or occasional racing classes. Other types last virtually unchanged for many years, retaining a traditional and perpetual appeal. Who has not lusted after a Vertue, Folkboat, Brixham trawler, or Falmouth Quay punt? Therefore, you should consider what the resale value of your boat is likely to be in, say, 3 years' time, when the children demand something a little bigger, faster and less stodgy.

I can recommend keeping an eye on the 'for sale' pages of yachting periodicals as the best way of keeping up with trends and prices. Prices are quoted for a great variety of craft and one can observe values changing. Often a boat will go out of production, when two things may happen. Either it immediately acquires a scarcity value and appreciates in price, which is not at all unusual, or, if it has proved unpopular or unsatisfactory, unsold models will appear month after month in the columns, with prices gradually dropping.

Experience and knowledge of different sorts of boats belonging to friends and club members, a watchful eye and ear around harbours and marinas, and a study of reports of boat trials and performances in magazines—all these will give you the feel of things and perhaps prevent you from making a poor choice.

There is a certain base level of price for most models of boat, which is modified by two factors—conditon and inventory. A well kept boat will survey better than one which has been neglected, and may prove a much better bargain even at a higher price. The inventory of a boat included in the selling price has already been touched on, but with secondhand boats it is very important to see what you are getting. A sound boat with an essential minimum of well found and maintained gear will serve you better than one fitted out with a multitude of gadgets and 'flimflams' which are probably both superfluous and highly priced.

Survey
New boats do not need a survey and can be referred back to the sellers should you uncover initial defects, though these can only be of workmanship or material. If you have bought a bad seaboat or a floating coffin, it will be your own responsibility for not having had an exhaustive trial sail before buying. With secondhand craft a full survey is essential, and you will have to pay for this yourself whether you buy or not.

Use the services of an independent and reputable surveyor. He will provide you with an objective report on the condition of the boat with recommendations of what needs to be done to bring her up to acceptable condition. In every case the list will be as long as your arm and seem highly discouraging at first glance, but do not despair. Many of his observations will be about minor matters which can be accepted and will not affect safety or performance. If the report shows major defects on which a significant amount of money needs to be spent, you should first think whether it is worth reviving such a hard-used and, probably, elderly boat. If so, insist on an equivalent reduction in the selling price, which has been agreed as 'subject to survey'. If the seller will not agree, you are obviously going to be out of pocket.

One thing a surveyor will not, and cannot be expected to do, is to commit himself on any valuation of the boat under survey. This is where you may have to rely not only on your own judgement but on that of experienced sailor friends. Among them may be some who know the boat concerned, or at any rate its type, and they can base a shrewd estimate of its worth on their own observation and the surveyor's report. Accept their advice and then make up your own mind. If you are entering the field of sailing for the first time, ask widely and see many craft before taking the plunge.

Insurance
As in every other field there is good and bad insurance in the marine world. Some firms specialise in yacht insurance and others sell it as part of a more generalised business. Once again enquire of the knowledgeable; among them will be some who have had dealing with insurance claims and will tell you of their experiences. Having chosen what you consider to be a suitable firm, get hold of a model policy and study it in fine detail before committing yourself.

Rates vary, though not very widely, and there are different rates for in-commission and laid-up periods. There are always clauses referring to damage caused when racing, so, if you intend only to cruise but get inveigled into club racing, have a look at your policy and get it adjusted if necessary. You will be asked to state your limits of cruising, and some areas are cheaper than others. If you intend to cruise in a very limited locality, as is likely in your first season or two, and to stay not more than a few miles offshore, it would be pointless to insure for cruising between Skaw Point and Cape St Vincent. On the other hand if you *are* so limited, do not sail intentionally outside your agreed area without first obtaining the concurrence of the firm, which will adjust your cover and charge accordingly.

Third party cover is absolutely essential and should be taken out for a good round sum—premiums are quite small. Should you injure someone or cause extensive damage to another boat, you could be in expensive trouble if not adequately covered.

Marine insurance expires on the stroke of the clock, unlike other forms of cover, under which you may still be insured after the precise date of expiry. Take no chances on this—it is not worth the risk of losing your boat. Marine insurance firms are remarkably good in settling justifiable claims fully and promptly, and it is only fair that they should be relieved of their onus once cover has terminated.

CHAPTER SIX

Safety Afloat

EQUIPMENT

A boat which *at any time* might be expected to meet with conditions that cause rolling, pitching and other motion making footing insecure should be fitted with guardrails all round. The minimum recommended height is 2ft, with an intermediate wire at half height. The bows should be enclosed by a pulpit of corresponding height against which a sitting man can rest his back when handling foresails. A stern pulpit (or pushpit if you prefer the word) gives added security to crew in the cockpit.

All places of work, such as the cockpit for helmsmen and sheet hands, foredeck and mast area for sailhandling and aft deck in the case of two-masted craft, should be equipped with stoutly backed and throughbolted rings into which harness can be clipped. Ancillary to these are removable fore and aft lines which can be conveniently tautened from pulpit to mast and thence aft along the coachroof, for use in heavy weather.

All openings in the hull should be fitted with seacocks, which should be closed unless actually in use. Seacocks and their fastenings must be of non-corrosive material such as bronze, gunmetal, stainless steel, hard plastic or nylon. If the last two are used, you should ensure that they are of reputable make and proven in use. It is not unknown for boats to be fitted with seacocks and fastenings of brass, but this is outrageous. They are a source of great danger, as the metal will sooner or later dezincify and crumble away.

Pipes leading to seacocks are normally clamped with jubilee

type clips. Although initially dearer, stainless or monel metal clips will not corrode and so not need periodic replacement. Badly rusted clips damage the pipes and are difficult to release in emergency.

Windows and other lights in superstructures are frequently found mounted in rubber gaskets. This type of fitting is not strong enough to take a heavy blow, and a sea coming aboard could dislodge the pane and admit a lot of water into the cabin. Panes are best clamped between an inner and an outer flange of suitable metal, such as marine aluminium or stainless steel, secured through with nuts and bolts. Whatever types of window are fitted can have removable shutters secured with butterfly nuts as an added security against very bad conditions.

At least two bilgepumps should be fitted—one to be operated from the cockpit and another to operate inside the cabin—for in heavy weather it may not be possible to get on deck in safety in order to pump bilges. An engine-driven pump will shift great quantities of water effortlessly, but such things can break down, and at least one manually operated pump should be installed. The larger the capacity of a pump to shift water the better, and the non-clogging diaphragm type is the best. It is very easy to clear if foreign matter does get sucked into it, but its valves are large enough to pass quite large bits of detritus without blockage. Vortex pumps clear vast quantities of water but have to be fitted right down in the bilge, and it calls for terrific manual effort to keep them rotating.

It is surprising how much water will get through an apparently closed companionway hatch. If this can be provided with a 'garage' (Fig 62) into which it slides, it will help to keep things dry below. Forehatches are often of poor design. Either they hinge backward and permit water to spray through them from the foredeck, or they are fully detachable and held in place with a lanyard or form of screwback. You should make sure that they are tightly sealed down on a gasket, and that there is no likelihood of their coming adrift if hit by a sea coming over the bows.

Tightly fitting canvas or PVC covers held down over hatches and skylights by means of a drawstring help keep water out.

A cockpit should be self-draining, but many are not. A non-

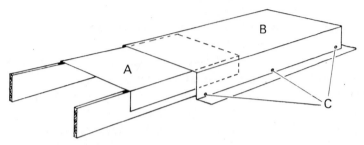

Fig 62 'Garage' for mainhatch
A Mainhatch
B GRP or wooden 'garage' affixed to coachroof
C Drainholes

draining cockpit is a nuisance on moorings, as a cover has to be put over it to keep out rain and spray, and a positive hazard at sea. Any such cockpit should have its own pump fitted to clear water taken in, although it is usually easier to use a bucket to get rid of the bulk of it. A filled cockpit will hold a great weight of water and bring the stern of a small boat well down. If large seas are running in from astern, the situation could become perilous. If it is possible to make the cockpit self-draining, even at the expense of comfort, by raising the level of the floor and fitting drains, this should be done. Most drains usually fitted are too small to be really effective; the minimum diameter should be 2in. If the cockpit cannot be wholly converted, it is often possible to fit a drain in a position above the waterline to drain out aft through the transom. A cockpit so fitted (Fig 63) will then empty itself of most of its contents, and the rest can be pumped out.

Gear
The items of gear listed below are regarded as essential for safety and should be carried *at all times*. Every venture afloat must be

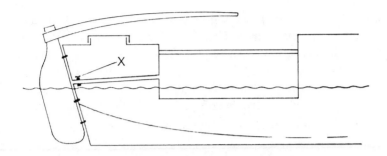

Fig 63 Partially self-draining cockpit. X=seacock

taken seriously, as so often conditions arise which turn a pleasant afternoon's jaunt into a struggle for survival.

Personal harness. One for each member of the crew, especially children.

Lifejackets. One for each crew member, able to support an unconscious person in a head-up position.

Lifebuoy. At least one, which should be fitted with a self-activating light.

Liferaft. Large enough to hold all crew and containing water, iron rations, compass and oars as a minimum. This can be omitted for inshore boats if an inflated dinghy is carried and can be launched within half a minute.

Flares. At least two each of the following: handheld red, handheld white, handheld orange smoke and parachute red.

Fire extinguishers. At least one near the galley and one near the engine.

Buckets. Two with lanyards for bailing and firefighting.

First Aid kit. As described later, complete with medical reference book.

Radar reflector. As large as can be carried. To be carried as high as possible in poor visibility and after dark.

In addition to these specific items other equipment really comes under the heading of safety gear but would normally be carried by any craft leaving moorings. These include anchor and cable, compass, charts, navigational gear and books, radio receiver for forecasts, barometer, toolkits for engine and for bosun's work (such as repairing sails), spare plugs, batteries, bulbs, shackles, screws, nuts and bolts, lengths of wire, adhesive tape, tin of grease, oil can and a pair of oars for emergencies.

AN EYE ON THE SKY

The approach and passage of an unfavourable weather system will bring a deterioration of conditions, with increasing wind, rising seas and a probability of rain and decreasing visibility. The rapidity of such a change depends on the intensity and size of a depression as well as its rate of movement as a mass. Conditions do not often change so suddenly as to preclude a period for intelligent preparation to meet the worsening weather, but squalls bring a sudden and dramatic change in wind strength and direction. Their approach can usually be deduced from observation of cloud formation and movements, and is often to be seen on the surface of the water, especially if they are carrying rain with them.

Broadcast forecasts of weather are usually pretty good, believe it or not, but utter reliance should not be placed on them for two main reasons. They are based on somewhat outdated information and a quickly moving minor depression may form and overtake the forecast. More importantly they cover wide areas, whereas some small areas like the Channel Islands and the coast of Brittany are subject to local weather which may have a more immediate effect on a boat than the synoptic conditions. In time you will learn to use your own observation and experience of similar conditions in the past to modify or complement a given outlook. Whatever a sailor may conclude about the immediate future, if he is wise he hopes for the best and prepares for the worst.

Snugging down

Gear and stores are automatically kept lashed and stowed on any well run boat but even so it is surprising how much tackle gets adrift in bad conditions. Close attention must be paid to snugging down above and below decks when a blow is coming. It is helpful if you allocate areas of work to individuals as part of their watch-keeping duties. They will then be familiar with that part of the ship they will have to snug down, when so ordered. Fore and aft lifelines should be rigged and the crew asked to wear harness when below in case of a deck call. The engine should be run briefly as a check on reliability, canvas covers should go on hatches, the liferaft be checked for security of lashing and ease of release, flares put ready to hand, and if possible hot drinks should be made and put into thermos flasks and at the same time some sandwiches cut.

The plot should be brought right up-to-date and every opportunity taken to confirm your position. If you are forced to heave-to or lie a'hull, it will be vital to know how your boat will drift or forereach.

Sail should be reduced by stages in ample time and not deferred until the vessel is overcanvassed and the task rendered heavy and hazardous. Few small cruisers are equipped with a trisail and storm jib; it is very doubtful if their cost would be warranted by the extremely infrequent occasions when they might be useful. When an absolute minimum of sail has to be carried—the last stage before heaving-to—you can use a small jib in the manner shown in Fig 64. This keeps the centre of effort low and permits a reasonable degree of manoeuvrability.

A carefully planned coastal passage should mean that you are unlikely to meet extreme conditions, but if you ever are unfortunate enough to do so, your boat may reach the stage of being unable to stand up to even a scrap of sail. You can then heave-to under minimal sail or hand it and lie under bare poles with tiller lashed down and the craft just bobbing around like a cork. As

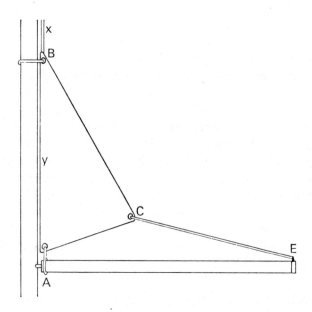

Fig 64 Makeshift storm gear (x=main halyard, y=luff of jib)

A Lash tack of sail round gooseneck
B Take bight of line through head cringle to hold sail close in to mast.
  Tauten luff wire by means of halyard winch or boom downhaul
C Sheet clew to end of boom. If leech is too slack, bring the sheet down to
  boom and lash it at required point between C and E. Use mainsheet as
  normally to control boom

long as she is watertight, she will remain buoyant and afloat, despite the inevitable misgivings of the crew, brought about by the noise and turmoil of wind and sea.

It is worth emphasising that a sound boat is in little danger off-shore. Providing the crew are prepared to sit out the blow, they will come to no real harm, even if they suffer from seasickness with the violent motion. One is shy of advising a course of action to be taken under extreme conditions, as circumstances will always be different and call for judgement at the time. Of one thing, however, I am quite sure. I would never turn and run for shelter unless I knew precisely where I was at the time, I was familiar with the intended refuge, and I was positive of getting there before conditions rendered my boat unmanoeuvrable. Proximity to a lee shore in bad weather is very hazardous, and you will never make anything to weather at such a time.

DAMAGE CONTROL

Major damage such as a great gaping hole knocked in the hull by a drifting baulk or hulk is mercifully rare. It is unlikely that anything constructive could be done about it and one would have to abandon ship. Hard weather can cause trivial to serious damage, and this can be roughly summarised as damage to sails, rigging or spars. Worst of all is hull damage, which may only become apparent through noticing that water is leaking aboard.

Leaks

Small holes and cracks should be plugged with rags or other such material, which then needs to be secured in place. With a wooden hull it is enough to cover the plugging with a layer of grease and a canvas patch closely tacked around the area of damage, preferably with brass or copper nails. Once the immediacy is past, an effort must be made to patch the leak from the outside of the hull with a similar greased canvas patch covered all round with a thin tacked-down copper plate (tingle).

Lost caulking or fastenings can cause water to be admitted between planks. This situation can be coped with from inside as a temporary measure, but if it is possible to plug seams or drive home fastenings from outside the hull, so much the better. If not, every effort should be made to relieve the hull of undue stress by sailing on the favouring tack, proceeding at reduced speed, heaving-to or going slow ahead on the auxiliary. The forces transmitted through sails, mast and rigging can be of a high order in heavy winds. Any action you can think of to reduce their effect may cut down the inflow of water.

GRP hulls present difficulties as it is not feasible to tack down a patch. The best expedient is to drive home a tapered plug covered with rag or rubber sheeting and to secure this against movement by simple shoring. Any bit of scrap timber can be used, but these are not usually to be found on plastic boats, so it will pay to carry a few random bits of softwood which can swiftly be whittled down into a tapered plug. GRP tends to craze outwards from a point of impact, so once the hole has been dealt with it may be necessary to plug seepage through lines of cracking with Seelastic or some similar stopping compound.

When the inflow has been halted, it is quite possible to be able to use resin, resin putty and a glassfibre patch to seal the hole. The prerequisite to this repair is that the surfaces should be quite dry, freed from grease and salt and abraded deeply to provide a keying surface. It might be possible to raise the affected area above the waterline by artificially heeling the boat. The surface can then be cleaned and dried by applying acetone or styrene, and scuffed up with the tang of a file and coarse sandpaper. Repair kits containing all the necessary materials can be had from moulders of GRP hulls, chandlers or specialist suppliers. You can make them up from separate items if you wish.

Dismasting

A mast can break or go over the side for many reasons, ranging from a compression fracture caused by undue stress to a simple rigging failure caused by a drawn splice or unsecured bottlescrew. It is a serious matter as it deprives you of motive power; this is not so bad if you have a reliable auxiliary and plenty of fuel. Much worse is the danger of hull damage or penetration by the mast and its fittings battering against the side in rough water. If the mast can be kept down to leeward—and it will probably fall that way—danger is reduced, but you should not let it trail astern with possible damage to rudder or propeller.

In the prevailing circumstances you will have to decide whether to cast it adrift or salvage it. If it can be got alongside and securely lashed to stanchions for use as jury rig later, so much the better, but the work can be arduous and hazardous. A wooden mast can be cut partially adrift and secured forward as a sea anchor of sorts, but a metal mast will sink and threaten the bottom of the hull. It then becomes imperative to get rid of it.

Stout wirecutters will make short work of standing rigging but are costly, heavy and difficult to keep free of rust. Larger craft may deem it worthwhile to carry a pair greased and sealed in a plastic bag against emergency, but it is just as effective to release all bottlescrews. These should at all times be kept free-running. A liberal application of anhydrous lanolin covered over with sticky tape will prevent them corroding, becoming encrusted with salt or otherwise seizing up.

Sails
Seams may become unstitched or fabric torn. Such damage is repairable by sewing and patching, and every boat should carry needles, thread, beeswax, a sailmaker's palm and a man who can use them to effect. The definitive book on the subject is the *Admiralty Sailmakers' Handbook* (BR 2176).

Rigging
Well maintained and regularly inspected rigging should not fail but it can happen at times. If splices draw out or swagings fail, temporary repairs can be effected by using bulldog clamps (Fig 65). A supply of these in the appropriate sizes should be kept aboard, together with a small adjustable spanner to tighten them. Parted rigging will leave gaps which can be spanned by prepared pendants made up of suitable wire. There are many ways of stropping wires together, and an easy one is shown using thimbled pendants and bulldog clips (Fig 66)

NIGHTFALL
Darkness restricts vision and consequently movement, so that physical precautions against accident and danger by day need to be intensified by night. For example, while optional on a calm day, harness should always be worn at night, for a man overboard

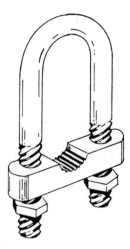

Fig 65   Bulldog clip

without one will be lucky to be recovered. Strict attention to watchkeeping is needed so that the crew will not be exposed to the effects of cold and fatigue. It may be inadvisable to leave one man on watch; should an emergency arise he might not be able to leave the helm to rouse persons soundly asleep below.

Vision

Bright lights should not be allowed to shine into the eyes of the watch on deck as this will affect their ability to discern traffic and other lights abroad. Saloon lights should be screened and the compass light reduced to the minimum needed for steering. Chart-table lights are best tinted red or orange, which colours

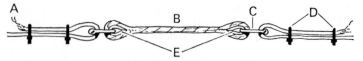

Fig 66   Repairing rigging

A Parted wire doubled back   D Bulldog clips
B Pendant   E Thimbles spliced in
C Pin shackle

have little detrimental effect on night vision. The use of spreader or deck lights is not called for under normal conditions; even on the darkest night there will be enough illumination to enable the deck to be worked. If the inboard edges of the toerail are painted a light colour, they will clearly define a danger limit. Similarly, it is of great advantage to emphasise the position of guardrails and points of attachment for harness clips.

Night rig
It is essential to have an all-round unobstructed view from the helm at night, so very low-cut foresails should not be set. Unhandy at the best of times, spinnakers cannot be watched and trimmed successfully in the dark, and they also restrict manoeuvring to an unacceptable degree. An automatic reduction of sail at nightfall is not needed in settled weather, but such action should be thought about if there is a possibility of any deterioration in conditions.

If thought advisable, you can reduce sail area, by reefing if necessary, to the maximum amount which can be easily handled by the watch on deck without need to disturb sleepers. It is a wise precaution if you are in any sort of doubt, but should not be carried to extremes or your passages will be unduly retarded.

Lights at sea
Helmsmen, and preferably all crew on watches, should be familiar with the various combinations of lights to be met with at sea. The more common ones can be memorised, but there will be occasions when you encounter unfamiliar configurations and will need to know their purport.

For easy reference, these are set out in the Appendix, together with the less complex ones. They are all prescribed by the Collision Rules, so that if you see lights that do not conform to the Appendix, the probability is that they will be carried by naval craft on exercise. Under such circumstances it is well to watch their movements closely and to keep well clear of convergence.

Bearings of converging lights should be taken at frequent intervals. Remember that you cannot estimate their distance from a single observation. Distant powerful lights will often seem nearer than closer dim ones. If there is the remotest possibility of convergence, you will be wise to alter course and keep out of trouble. In doing so, make large and positive alterations to course so that you clearly signal your movement and intentions to the other craft.

You must be discernible.

Your own lights should be as powerful as possible, and correctly mounted and screened. Much trouble is occasioned to themselves and others by boats carrying misaligned port and starboard lights (Fig 67).

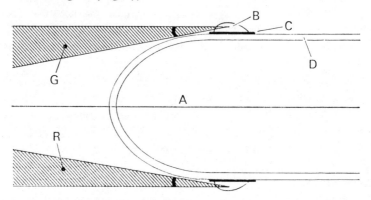

Fig 67   Misaligned lights—I

A Fore and aft line   D Pulpit rail
B Streamlined light   G Green light visible over this arc
C Mounting plate   R Red light visible over this arc

Lightboards of the proper pattern can seldom be fitted in the restricted space on small craft, but attention must be given to the need for some form of effective screening. Many owners remain unaware that *both* lights can be seen from a considerable angle on either side of the fore and aft line. This is very dangerous. A critical scrutiny of your own lights from a position ahead of the boat and slightly to either side will show up faults. Misaligned overtaking lights are also not in accordance with the Rules, but this is not quite so dangerous. None the less such a fault should be corrected.

Radar reflector
A radar reflector should always be carried where shipping is likely to be encountered; essential by night and in low visibility, it is an added insurance against a bad lookout by day aboard

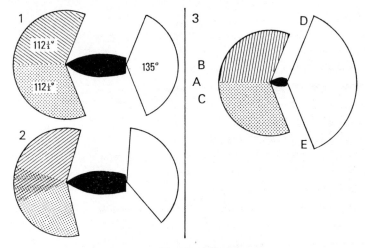

Fig 68   Misaligned lights—II

1 Lights correctly adjusted
2 Maladjusted lights—overlapping arcs, etc
3 Results of adjustment—good and bad

Seen from	With lights in order	With lights maladjusted
A	Red and green	Red and green
B	Green alone	Red and green
C	Red alone	Red and green
D	Green suddenly changing to white	White and green, then changing to white
E	Red changing to white	None visible, then white

ships. To be effective it must be as large as possible—14in from corner to corner is the minimum—and carried as high as possible.

One which is lower than about 10ft above the waterline may not register on a ship's screen owing to surface clutter. This is increased as seas grow, and many vessels have radar equipped with a clutter cut-off, which effectively stops their surveillance of several feet above sealevel. The efficiency of a reflector depends not only on its size but on the accuracy of the rightangles between the surfaces of the plates. It pays to buy a properly engineered model and not to knock it about. Collapsible models are available and very suitable for stowing on small craft when not needed.

Flares
If despite good lights and a radar reflector you do not seem to have been observed by an approaching vessel, and there is possibility of collision, wake him up. A white flare will draw immediate attention to your position and a few of these should be handy to the cockpit, protected from damp. They can usefully be clipped just inside the main hatch.

Read the operating instructions carefully on purchase and see that all crew know how to ignite them. Make sure that they point well away from your sails, downwind and over the rail. They should be renewed annually.

A Very pistol and white cartridges come in useful at times. You can fire at an offending merchantman with a real hope of rousing his lookout, but try to avoid landing a cartridge on the deck of an oiltanker. Red cartridges can be used as distress flares, and are an acceptable substitute for parachute flares, although they burn for a shorter period.

FIRE
Minimising risk
Fires usually arise from the ignition of engine fuel or galley fat. Gas will usually cause an explosion which may be followed by fire. The prevention of fire is of paramount importance, as once it takes hold of the hull structure, danger is acute. GRP will burn fiercely once ignited and may prove impossible to extinguish.

It is possible to mould hulls in fire-resistant resin, but this is not usual.

It should be an inviolable routine never to take inflammable liquids below decks except for small amounts needed to fill a paraffin or spirit stove, or the integral tank of a small engine. A large funnel should be used to transfer liquids, and spillage sponged up immediately. Containers should be taken back to their above-deck stowage as soon as you are finished with them.

Built-in fuel tanks should have filler and breather caps above decks, and there should be a programmed inspection of tanks and pipes for leakage, fracture or abrasion. Copper pipes are prone to become brittle with age and vibration, and then may develop haircracks. Somewhere along their length they should have a looped coil to allow for expansion and contraction.

Gas cylinders should be stowed in an above-deck locker with a vent leading overboard. The main cock should be kept closed unless the stove or other apparatus is in use. After use, stove taps should be left open until the cylinder has been shut off and the gas in the pipes allowed to burn out. Flexible pipes should be used to carry gas, and their end connections inspected closely for slackness and seepage of gas.

Extinguishers

Extinguishers should be as large as can conveniently be carried, since ignited fuel spreads over a considerable area and the whole of it will need to be doused. It must be possible to get at an extinguisher from both above and below decks; it is sensible to have one in the vicinity of the galley, one near the engine and one in the cockpit. Choice is wide, and effective extinguishers can contain foam, powder, carbon dioxide or an extinguishant liquid. Trichlorethylene should be avoided, as it can give rise to the formation of poisonous gases when used in certain circumstances.

An addition to firefighting equipment should be an asbestos blanket kept near the galley. This will smother the flames from grease or cooking fat ignited in frying pans without fouling the entire area with extinguishant. Galley fires are not infrequent occurrences, and the cook will be protected from blazing fats to a great extent if he wears oilskin trousers when about his task.

If clothing does catch fire, the wearer should be thrown down and rolled into a blanket, sleeping bag, sail or other thing to smother the flames. Later he should be stripped and examined for burns, then treated for them and for shock.

Water will immediately extinguish the flames from methylated or other stove spirit, as alcohol mixes with water. It should, however, never be used in connection with petrol or paraffin fires, as these substances will float on it while continuing to burn, and be spread to other areas.

MAN OVERBOARD

This is a major disaster and must be treated as such at all times, even though there may not seem to be any immediate danger to the man in the water. His rescue must override all other considerations short of losing the boat and the remaining crew. The situation will seldom arise if all crew habitually wear their personal harness, but it can happen. The rescue routine recommended, or a similar procedure suitable to your own circumstances, should be practised by day and by night.

Immediate action

On the alarm being sounded, the nearest man should hurl a lifebuoy as near as possible to the man in the water, without hitting him. He may be able to swim to it. No lifebuoy is of the slightest use if it is lashed down, no matter how lightly. It should be carried resting in a pocket from which it can be instantly lifted clear, and it should be equipped with a self-activating light.

All on board who can do so should report 'I can see him'. The skipper or watchkeeper should nominate one of them to keep pointing at the man in the water, whose head will appear small and be extremely difficult to pick up once it is lost sight of.

Everyone else should try to avoid obstructing the view of the pointer, who may have to move around the deck as the boat changes course.

If the boat is driving fast, the helmsman should note his heading, log reading and the time. Some distance may be covered before the boat can be turned round, and this will have to be recovered on a reciprocal course. Unless very strong, the stream effect can be disregarded. The reciprocal can be sailed direct unless the reversed course is into the wind, when the boat should be short tacked equally on either side of the reciprocal baseline.

If the lifebuoy has no light, or it has failed, you will have to listen carefully for the man overboard once the distance has been covered back to his area. An engine in use may have to be shut off for the purpose. At such times extremely careful navigation is essential to keep the boat from getting out of earshot area, and the navigator on duty must take over the direction of the ship.

Recovery
The boat should be brought stationary a couple of feet to windward of the swimmer, to afford him as much lee as possible. You will have to watch that you do not drive down on him, but if you come up on his leeward side, he could be dashed against the side by a wave.

If he is unconscious, or cannot reach the rail unaided for any reason, a man will have to go over the side to him and *must* himself be secured to a line. Both men can be brought alongside, and a line got round the rescued man at once.

It can be very difficult to get an exhausted or unconscious man over the rail in even flat conditions. If there is anything of a lop about, you must be careful that he is not injured in the process. A purchase attached to the end of the boom will often lift him enough to swing him inboard if he cannot be lifted in. Alternatively he can be got into the tender and thence into the boat, and an inflatable is better than a wooden dinghy for this purpose. The tender should be secured to the boat by means of its painter, but any men in it should also have lines around them secured inboard. It is bad enough having one man adrift without his rescuers being in danger of joining him.

FIRST AID

The coastal sailor will not have to treat scurvy or tropical yaws, but sailing has special afflictions to be coped with at sea. The notes which follow are brief, and hopefully helpful, but cannot take the place of a good medical reference book, which should be carried aboard every cruising boat. First aid is intended to treat a victim until he can be got to expert medical attention, if this is needed; often it is not and the normal shoreside attention for minor upsets suffices to allow the passage to continue uninterrupted.

First Aid kit

A First Aid kit is as essential to every boat as is the familiar medicine cabinet to a home. It should be kept dry in a container clearly marked and easily accessible. Suggested contents are as follows:

1. Bandages of various widths and lengths, including elastic ones for sprains. These can be fixed with safety pins, pieces of sticky plaster, Sellotape or just split and tied.
2. Adhesive plaster, both a roll and an assortment of Elastoplast or similar patches. This stuff is quickly affected by seawater and comes adrift unless it is kept in place by taking a couple of turns over it with Sellotape or sticky boat tape, a roll of which should be kept in the kit.
3. A roll of cotton wool for wiping wounds and making up pads for compresses.
4. Seasickness pills. I shall say a word about these later.
5. Aspirins and Alkaseltzer.
6. Dettol or other disinfectant.
7. A clinical thermometer.
8. Stainless steel scissors.
9. A small bottle of brandy.
10. An eyebath and eyewash.
11. A surgical needle and thread.
12. Aludrox tablets.

SERIOUS INJURY OR ILLNESS

In the case of broken bones, loss of blood, concussion and other serious affairs, in addition to doing as much as you can to stop things getting worse, you will need to comfort and reassure your patient. Expert help is essential and the boat must immediately be headed for the nearest haven or to a passing vessel if you are offshore and it is an urgent case. Signal 'W' (· – –)—I need medical assistance.

Broken bones

A fractured limb should be padded as comfortably as possible and immobilised by lashing it to a splint of timber or metal. A broken leg can be lashed to the sound one or an arm to the trunk with long bandages or torn-up sheets. If a bone protrudes through the skin, it should be covered with a sterilised dressing before immobilising it. If a bloodvessel has been punctured, it is essential to stem the bleeding as a first measure. The patient should be made as warm and comfortable as can be, and lashed into a berth if the boat is moving about much.

Bleeding

You can usually stem bleeding from cuts and gashes by putting a pad over them and maintaining pressure on it until the blood clots. Pads can be held in place with a firm bandage or a length of Sellotape. Really deep cuts and wounds will gape open and the edges need to be drawn together before pressure is put on them. In bad cases you will have to stitch them up. The needle and thread should be sterilised with Dettol or some other disinfectant before use, and the stitches inserted individually. Tie them with a reef knot and cut off the long ends. The area of the wound is often quite numb at the time, but in any case stitching is not very painful and the patient should be prepared to endure it. Blood frightens a lot of people, so they need considerable reassurance that they are going to recover. They may go into shock.

Burns
Burns are best left alone except for covering with a loose dressing. They are painful, but messing about with them may make matters worse, and if they are extensive, medical attention is the only way of being sure that they are not followed by permanent disfigurement.

Shock
Fractures, burns and bleeding can cause a patient to go into shock. He will go pale, sweat and tremble and may collapse. Keep him warm and comfortable and reassure him. Give him sparingly hot sweet tea or other non-alcoholic drinks.

Concussion
Concussion is always to be treated seriously, and anyone who has received a blow to the head, especially if it has caused even a brief period of unconsciousness, should be kept warm and recumbent until he can be got to a doctor. Shock may not follow concussion, and very often a sufferer will express a desire to get up and about; this should be resisted.

Internal complaints
People may suddenly develop perforated ulcers or other intestinal disorders resulting in pain and incapacity. It is unwise to give them anything to drink, and treatment must be confined to comfort and warmth pending medical attention.

ARTIFICIAL RESPIRATION
Suffocation can be brought about by drowning, inhalation of exhaust gases or obstructions to the air passages. Lack of oxygen causes permanent brain damage if the air supply is not restored pretty quickly, so that speed of resuscitation is paramount. There are many ways of applying artificial respiration, but the so-called 'kiss of life' is probably simpler than most to use.

First make sure that throat and air passages are not obstructed by foreign matter, such as seaweed, and that the tongue has not fallen backwards; if it has, pull it out. If a drowned man is bubbling water, he should be turned face down for a brief period to clear his air passages.

Lay the patient on his back and straighten his air passages by pushing up his chin to force the head back. Pinch his nose shut and, putting your mouth to his, breath into it until you see his chest inflate. Take your mouth clear and his chest should relax. Repeat this action about nine or ten times a minute until he starts to breath unaided. You may have to continue this for quite a long time, even in shifts, but the respiration must continue until it is quite certain that he is not going to recover.

This will only be when his heart has stopped beating, and you can check on this by feeling his pulse or listening to his chest. If the heart stops beating while you are breathing into his lungs, all is not lost if you can get it to restart.

While you continue with the breathing routine, another man should lift his legs in a vertical position and prop them there. Hard pressure on the breastbone, just above the solar plexus, should be applied at about the frequency of a normal heartbeat—slightly more than once a second. The combination of respiring and stimulating the heart may revive the patient if continued for long enough.

Take care if breathing into children not to injure their lungs by overinflation; gentler and more rapid respiration is necessary.

A recovered patient is in urgent need of hospital treatment and should be kept warm. Lay him on his side with the head facing slightly downwards and keep a constant watch on him. His stomach may be full of water and he must not be allowed to vomit it up and breath it into his lungs.

MINOR MATTERS

Seasickness

This can vary from a mild and non-recurrent attack to severe prostration with racking vomiting and even loss of the will to live. Fortunately all sufferers recover when motion has ceased. They frequently want to stay up on deck where they cannot look after themselves, get wet and cold, and are in danger of falling overboard. Cold and wet will aggravate their condition and can cause a dangerous drop in body temperature. Get them to lie warm below with a bucket alongside; they will probably complain, but it is for the best.

The sickness can usually be averted by taking such drugs as dramamine or avomine a short time before setting sail and continuing the dosage as prescribed for as long as is necessary. Different drugs have different side effects, but the main one is drowsiness. It is pointless to ask people suffering from this to try to stay alert, so get to know the effects on your crew beforehand, especially if you will be shorthanded.

Sprains and strains
Joints and spine can be affected by awkward and heavy stresses. Joints can be firmly bandaged with an elastic bandage, taking care not to interfere with the blood circulation, but an affected back is best dealt with by keeping the sufferer flat on his back as long as necessary. A slipped disc in the spine or neck can cause pain of varying severity and, although there is no danger to life, it is as well to get the patient ashore for treatment as soon as possible.

Sunburn
Reflection of the sun's rays from the water, brightwork and sails in addition to direct contact can very quickly cause severe sunburn. It is not to be taken lightly. Bad sunburn can cause shock. Prevention is better than cure and light clothing should be worn at all times. Mild cases can be soothed with calamine lotion, but severe burning is the same as any other type of burn and should be treated accordingly.

Exposure
Wet and cold can seriously affect physical and mental performance, and is best prevented by a good system of watchkeeping
and sensible use of protective clothing. Older people become
progressively more susceptible to the effects of exposure and, if
you have any aboard, keep an eye on them for shivering or slowed
reactions. The cure is a rub down, dry clothing, a warm bunk
and hot drinks. Avoid alcohol.

Coughs, colds, 'flu and the like
Just treat these as you would ashore, but a small boat is no place
for a man with a temperature. He needs to be landed for attention. Better still, try to persuade him to stay ashore in the first
instance.

Minor cuts and grazes
Salt water, if clean, is a good disinfectant and minor injuries
are unlikely to become infected. They can be covered with a
small bandage or plaster and otherwise ignored.

Postcript

Sailing is meant to be enjoyed, but fundamentally it is a serious business. A sailor has to learn to live with the uncaring implacability of the sea and ignores or underrates its potential danger at his peril. He and his boat must be equipped and ready to respond adequately to whatever the sea may demand of them at any moment. A skipper bears a weight of responsibility for all people on board and to other seafarers around him, no matter how lightly he chooses to carry it. To this end he needs the confidence bred of learning and the skills developed by practice. The watchwords are knowledge and self-reliance.

Today's owner will likely do most of his own maintenance, fitting-out, navigation and handling. If he knows precisely what he is about and is scrupulous in all he does, his time at sea will be happy and rewarding. The sea will not long tolerate such things as wishful thinking, indecision and carelessness; the price of survival is eternal vigilance. Eyes that appraise the set of a sail must always be alert for the broken stitch, approaching lights, snagged rope, error in navigation and the thousand other little things which, unobserved or unremedied, can snowball into crisis.

I make no apology to those who may read into these pages an undue emphasis on safety afloat, but merely say that prudence is not timidity nor caution craven. Of course, sailing can never be wholly safe and would be dull if it were. At times one has no alternative to taking a calculated risk, but penalties will sooner or later be exacted for foolhardiness and bravado. The essence of carefree sailing is constant unobtrusive prudence.

Lights at Sea

In this series of diagrams the plain circles indicate white lights, the dotted circles green lights and the black circles red lights.

Head-on	Oblique approach	Abeam	Stern-to

Power-driven vessel, under 150ft in length, under way

Head-on	Oblique approach	Abeam	Stern-to

Power-driven vessel, over 150ft in length, under way

Head-on	Oblique approach	Abeam	Stern-to

Power-driven vessel towing or pushing another vessel where the total length of the assembly is less than 600ft

Head-on	Oblique approach	Abeam	Stern-to

Power-driven vessel towing or pushing another vessel where the total length of the assembly exceeds 600ft

Head-on	Oblique approach	Abeam	Stern-to

Vessel under way but not under command

Head-on	Oblique approach	Abeam	Stern-to

Vessel not under command and not under way

Head-on	Oblique approach	Abeam	Stern-to

Vessel, under way, engaged on laying or picking up submarine cables or navigational marks. Give good clearance and regard her as not fully under command

Head-on	Oblique approach	Abeam	Stern-to

Vessel, not under way, engaged on laying or picking up submarine cables or navigational marks

Head-on	Oblique approach	Abeam	Stern-to

Vessel, under way, engaged on minesweeping operations. Do not close to within ½ mile of such a vessel from astern or the side on which the indicating light is exhibited

Head-on	Oblique approach	Abeam	Stern-to

Vessel, not under way, engaged on minesweeping operations. Give good clearance

Head-on	Oblique approach	Abeam	Stern-to

Sailing vessel under way

Head-on	Oblique approach	Abeam	Stern-to

Sailing vessel under way carrying optional addition to navigation lights

Head-on	Oblique approach	Abeam	Stern-to
⊛ ●	●	●	○

Vessel being towed. If observed, look for vessel ahead carrying towing lights; there will be a towline between them

Head-on	Oblique approach	Abeam	Stern-to
⊛ ●	●	●	

Vessel being pushed

Head-on	Oblique approach	Abeam	Stern-to
○ ○ ⊛ ● ⊛ ●	○ ○ ● ●	○ ○ ● ●	○ ○

Group of vessels being pushed, including pusher

Head-on	Oblique approach	Abeam	Stern-to
○ ⊛ ●	○ ●	○ ●	○ ○

Pilot vessel, under way and on duty. She will also show one or more flare-up lights at intervals not exceeding 10 minutes, or a bright white light in lieu

Head-on	Oblique approach	Abeam	Stern-to
O	O	O	O

Pilot vessel, on duty but not under way. She will show a flare-up light, or bright white light in lieu, at intervals of not more than 10 minutes

Head-on	Oblique approach	Abeam	Stern-to
O	O	O	O
O	O	O	
			O

Pilot vessel, on duty at anchor. She will also show flare-up lights, or a bright white light in lieu, at intervals of not more than 10 minutes

Head-on	Oblique approach	Abeam	Stern-to
◉	◉	◉	◉
O	O	O	O
◉ ●	●	●	O

Trawler, under way, engaged in fishing

Head-on	Oblique approach	Abeam	Stern-to
◉	◉	◉	◉
O	O	O	O
O	O	O	
◉ ●	●	●	O

Trawler, under way, engaged in fishing

Head-on	Oblique approach	Abeam	Stern-to

Trawler, not under way

Head-on	Oblique approach	Abeam	Stern-to

Fishing vessel, other than trawler, under way and engaged in fishing

Head-on	Oblique approach	Abeam	Stern-to

Fishing vessel, other than trawler, not under way

Head-on	Oblique approach	Abeam	Stern-to

Fishing vessel, other than trawler, under way with gear lying out more than 500ft to the side, indicated by the additional white light

Head-on   Oblique approach   Abeam   Stern-to

Fishing vessel, other than trawler, not under way but with gear lying out more than 500ft to the side, indicated by the additional white light

Head-on   Oblique approach   Abeam   Stern-to

Vessel, under 150ft in length, at anchor

Head-on   Oblique approach   Abeam   Stern-to

Vessel, over 150ft in length, at anchor

Head-on   Oblique approach   Abeam   Stern-to

Vessel, under 150ft in length, aground

Head-on	Oblique approach	Abeam	Stern-to

Vessel, over 150ft in length, aground

List of Recommended Reading

Admiralty. *Manual of Navigation*, vol 1
Admiralty. *Manual of Seamanship*, vols 1 & 2
Admiralty. *Sailmakers' Handbook*
Baader, J. *The Sailing Yacht*
Blewitt, M. *Navigation for Yachtsmen*
Bowker & Budd. *Make your own Sails*
Bramham, K. *Handyman Afloat and Ashore*
Day, C. L. *Knots and Splices*
Delmar-Morgan, E. *Small Craft Engines and Equipment*
Desoutter, D. *Small Boat Cruising*
Du Plessis, H. *Fibreglass Boats*
Fox, Uffa. *Sailing Boats*
Fraser, B. *At Home in Deep Waters*
Haward, P. *All Seasons' Yachtsman*
Hiscock, E. *Cruising under Sail*
Hiscock, E. *Voyaging under Sail*
Illingworth, J. *Further Offshore*
Marchaj, C. J. *Sailing Theory and Practice*
Proctor, I. *Sailing: Wind and Current*
Rantzen, M. J. *English Channel Tides*
Reed, T. *Yachtmaster* series, vol 1—*Coastal Navigation*
Watts, A. *Instant Weather Forecasting*
Wickam, J. *Motor Boats and Motor Boating*

Index

Index